The Four-Step Plan to Rise
Above Unseen Influences

Mental Reprogramming: Through the learned technique of self-hypnosis, you can heighten your motivation, making your subconscious work *with* your conscious desires—you can even learn to program your dreams!

Diet and Nutrition: Affluence and technology result in tasty poisons for a human body genetically conditioned to whole, natural foods. Learn a new way of eating—a new way to health and energy.

Aerobic Exercise: The body not used deteriorates. Regain and maintain your body with jogging, bicycling, swimming and walking!

Self-actualization: Become all you are capable of being. Accept the warmth and joy in life; detach from negativity. Rise above external manipulation and fear.

LEARN THE ELEVEN HUMAN RIGHTS . . .

. . . which allow expression, oppose repression and encourage assertion—rights you will deny no one, and demand for yourself!

Books by Dick Sutphen

Past Lives, Future Loves
Unseen Influences
You Were Born Again to Be Together

Published by POCKET BOOKS

DICK SUTPHEN

UNSEEN INFLUENCES

PUBLISHED BY POCKET BOOKS NEW YORK

My thanks to Marcia Miller for permission to use her real name in the case histories. In all other case histories, the names have been changed to retain the anonymity of the subject.

Another *Original* publication of POCKET BOOKS

POCKET BOOKS, a Simon & Schuster division of GULF & WESTERN CORPORATION 1230 Avenue of the Americas, New York, N.Y. 10020

Copyright © 1982 by Dick Sutphen

All rights reserved, including the right to reproduce this book or portions thereof in any form whatsoever. For information address Pocket Books, 1230 Avenue of the Americas, New York, N.Y. 10020

ISBN: 0-671-82604-2

First Pocket Books printing May, 1982

10 9 8 7 6 5 4 3 2 1

POCKET and colophon are trademarks of Simon & Schuster.

Printed in the U.S.A.

It is time to
reject the unseen influences
and direct your own destiny

CONTENTS

SECTION I
Mental and Physical Unseen Influences

Manifest Potentials   10
Past Experiences   15
Unrecognized Altered States   26
Cumulative Effects   37
The Body/Mind Connection   50
Body Types   60
Brain-Wave Similarities and Psychic Input   65
Body Rhythms   73
Positive and Negative Ions   83
Programming Dreams   90

SECTION II
The Metaphysical Influences

Metaphysical Potentials   100
Past and Parallel Lives   112
Astrology   119
Psychometric Atmospheres   128
Energy Vampirism   138
Psychic Attack   144
Other Influences   153

SECTION III
Rising Above the Unseen Influences

The Power of the Mind   156

A Four-Step Plan to Rise
   Above the Unseen Influences   166

About the Author   191

Section I

MENTAL AND PHYSICAL UNSEEN INFLUENCES

Chapter 1

MANIFEST POTENTIALS

Jerry

"They conducted just about every test known to contemporary medical science and didn't find a thing. I'm supposed to be in perfect health," Jerry said, waving an envelope of test results. His voice was frustrated, and he made no attempt to hide his disappointment. "I've been brain-scanned and probed. . . . They had me drink strange concoctions and then X-rayed me upside down and downside up. Blood tests and urine tests proved nothing. I was hooked up to all sorts of electronic devices that gave me a clean bill of health. The only problem is I feel lousy."

"What are your symptoms?" I asked.

"I am always tired and depressed, so I started to do some exercises after I watched a television show about the evils of sedentary living. The exercises just made me light-headed and dizzy, so I stopped. Then my kidneys started hurting, and I got migraine headaches all the time. Each day it seemed my batteries ran down a little more."

"Did you see anyone other than your medical doctor?"

"Only the other doctors he sent me to for tests, and the hospital personnel. My doctor thinks it might be mental and suggests I see a psychiatrist."

"Did anyone ever ask you about your diet or speak to you of nutrition?"

"No."

"Was one of your tests a Six-Hour Glucose Tolerance Test? They would have had you drink a very sweet substance, and then continued to check you periodically for six hours."

"No. Don't tell me I missed one!"

"Living in southern California, you are close to the beach. Do you like to go to the beach?"

"What's that have to do with this?"

"It is a very valid question, believe me. Do you like to go to the beach?"

"I love it. It's one of the few times I really feel alive . . . probably because I can unwind and relax in that environment."

This is part of a conversation with Jerry Celina, which transpired while my wife Trenna and I were in Los Angeles conducting a seminar on "Creating a New Reality." I'm a writer, lecturer, and hypnotist, and I encourage mental reprogramming, psychic understanding, and an awareness of the importance of proper nutrition and exercise. I am not a doctor and cannot prescribe, but my involvement with individuals and case histories has provided me with an extensive background in human problems, which often can be easily resolved once the proper therapies are undertaken.

Since traditional physicians had been unable to successfully diagnose Jerry's problem, I recommended that he see a naturopathic physician and nutritionist. I also advised that he check on the possibility of other unseen influences (environmental, nutritional, psychic, etc.) before labeling the problem a mental one.

As was soon to be revealed, there was nothing mentally wrong with Jerry. Rather, he was being negatively influenced by factors not traditionally considered by health-care specialists. For example, Jerry's response to the question about the beach was a clue that he might be sensitive to ions, electrically charged particles that fill the air. Seventy-five percent of the population are substantially—and negatively—influenced by an overdose of positive ions. Some of the symptoms of sensitivity to positive ions are depression, anxiety, and respiratory ailments. Conversely, a person who is ion-sensitive will react to an environment high in negative ions—such as the beach, pine forests, or open country meadows—by feeling increased energy, calmness, and tranquility.

Jerry was highly sensitive to positive ions, with which he was frequently surrounded by way of dry California winds. When he exposed himself to a negatively ionized environment, the negative effects disappeared.

The naturopath found that Jerry had a rather severe case of hypoglycemia (low blood sugar) and was obviously on his way to worse health due to the physically degenerative diet of refined flour and sugar-based foods on which he was living. Few doctors yet understand or even check for hypoglycemia, all because it is a new disease, generally created by the foods we eat. The naturopathic physician also suggested physical exercise as an important aspect of therapy.

A few months later, a note from Jerry arrived. "I would never have believed that such simple things were causing my problems, or that it was possible to feel this good." He explained that he had moved to Coos Bay, Oregon, and lived close to the sea. "Do we ever have negatively ionized air up here!" Becoming a health-food advocate and a bicycle enthusiast, he also revised his dietary and sedentary habits.

Adelle

One of every seven to ten people is a somnambulist. That means they can easily alter their state of consciousness to the deepest levels of hypnosis. Those levels are labeled, from lightest to deepest trance, as: beta, alpha, theta, and delta. The levels correspond to cycles-per-second of brain-wave activity, with delta showing the least activity on the EEG machine.

Although only 10% of the population can easily achieve the deepest levels of trance, I'm convinced after hypnotizing thousands of people that at least 25% of the population are capable of achieving a somnambulist level under certain conditions. This has its advantages and disadvantages.

There are several ways to determine whether you are a somnambulist. If you sleepwalk, you are probably a somnambulist. If you frequently "go on automatic" while you are driving and often find yourself in locations you don't remember having driven past, you may be a somnambulist. If you've ever been hypnotized and found yourself responding automatically to suggestions given by a hypnotist, you may be a somnambulist. If you are a somnambulist, any repetitive sound or motion can lull you into a trance, and the results can be disastrous.

In seminars, I often ask the audience how many of them have been involved in one-car accidents that they really didn't understand. During one seven-day seminar, I asked this question, and about twenty participants raised their hands. Over the next few days, I was able to observe these participants during hypnosis sessions; fifteen of them were somnambulists.

Adelle was one of the deepest-level subjects I'd ever hypnotized. During group-hypnosis sessions, she slipped into a deep-level trance a few seconds after I began the verbal body relaxation, which occurs five minutes prior to the beginning of any hypnosis induction. When I talked to her about the potential dangers of this situation, Adelle explained that after three bad accidents and a multitude of close calls, she had given up driving a car.

"Busy traffic keeps me alert," she said, "but the moment there is sparse traffic I just seem to drift away. It's impossible for me to drive out in the country, and I wouldn't consider getting behind the wheel at night. This was part of my decision to move to New York City, where everyone uses cabs for transportation."

Adelle is an extreme case, but she's only one of about 50,000,000 people who could slip into an altered state without realizing it.

Ryan

After living a responsible life as a family man and educator, Ryan Darthan, in his late forties, began acting strangely. His usual mellow personality gave way to an aggressiveness that was frequently accented by outbursts of extreme hostility. Major behavioral changes began to occur. For example, although Ryan was normally a conservative man monetarily, he purchased a new foreign car, which he couldn't afford, and hid it so his wife wouldn't know about it. Each morning he left his house, jogged to the top of the hill where the car was parked, and drove to work. When his wife and family were about to have him committed, Ryan's alert physician discovered that Ryan was allergic to salt. In addition to the hypertension, or high blood pressure, that is symptomatic of a salt allergy, there was a chemical imbalance that explained Ryan's strange behavior. He was put on a salt-free diet and within days became his old self again.

I have used these preceding examples as an introduction to the world of mental and physical unseen influences. The following chapters will examine nine unseen influences in detail.

Chapter 2

PAST EXPERIENCES

As I explained in my earlier book, *Past Lives, Future Loves,* our subconscious mind stores the memories of all our experiences (if you believe in reincarnation, that would also include all of your past-life experiences) in the same way that a computer stores programming input. All of your problems and afflictions, talents and abilities are the result of past programming of your subconscious computer. Thus, past experiences are definitely an unseen influence.

> Cindy Putnaham
> Age: 32
> Married
> Executive Secretary
> Problem: fear of dogs

"Is there anything that you can do with hypnosis to help me get over this problem?" she asked. "Over the weekend my husband and I attended a pool party given by his boss. Everything was fine. I was having a very good time until someone let the host's prize Irish Setter into the backyard. At first I just froze, hoping it would stay away, but it didn't. When it approached me, I fell down trying to get away from it. I guess the dog thought I was playing or something, because it jumped on me—it wasn't mean . . . just playful, but I lost control and started crying and screaming. It was terribly embarrassing, especially for my husband. I'm sure you can imagine the apologies, explanations, and strange looks from all the other guests."

"Have you always been afraid of dogs?" I asked.

"I don't know about always, but I have been since my early teen years. I don't know why it started. I've never had any bad experiences with dogs."

We discussed several potential techniques to overcome Cindy's phobia: reprogramming hypnosis, regressive hypnosis, and behavioral psychology. I favor positive reprogramming techniques, for they are often successful if the subject is willing to devote a few minutes daily to giving himself or herself positive suggestions via prerecorded reprogramming hypnosis tapes.

"But maybe it is something from a past life," Cindy said. "Wouldn't it be better to use regressive hypnosis first to find the cause of the problem?"

"If you'd prefer, Cindy. The cause isn't always that easy to discover in a single session or even during multiple regression sessions. Thus, it could take more sessions, and if we do find the cause, that doesn't ensure that the knowledge will eliminate your fear of dogs."

"But I've read in your books about several situations in which understanding the cause of the fear was enough to release the person from its effects," she responded hopefully.

"Sure, it does happen sometimes—but that's the exception, not the rule."

Cindy wanted to try regression first. When I use regressive-hypnosis techniques to locate the source of a problem, I simply instruct the subject to go back to the cause without saying anything about past lives. Part of the induction suggestion is: "You are in a deep, deep, hypnotic sleep, and you are going to go back to the origin of your fear of dogs. . . . I am going to count backward from five to one, with special instructions, and on the count of one you will see yourself in the situation that created your present-day fear of dogs."

The instructions were given, and the deeply hypnotized woman rested peacefully in the recliner lounge.

Q. I now want you to speak up and tell me what you see and what you are doing at this time.

A. Just a-walkin' in the corn. (Her voice sounded very young.)

Q. How old are you? Can you tell me your age?

A. I'm this many.

Q. I'm afraid I don't have my glasses with me, and I can't see very well. How many is that?

A. Five. Pretty soon I'll be six.

Q. Pretty soon?

A. Well, it will be a while.

Q. Can you tell me your name? I'd like to know your name.

A. Cindy Put . . . naham, and I live at 514 Grover Street.

Q. Is that where you are now?

A. Oh, no . . . this is my gram's. It's a long ways from my house. Mommy and I are staying with Gram for a week.

Q. What are you doing now?

A. Just walking along with Sally, and it's really hard to even see the sky 'cause of all the corn.

Q. Is Sally your friend?

A. No, silly . . . she is my doll. You knew that.

Q. That was silly of me, wasn't it? Well, is anything else happening right now?

A. Nope . . . old Scruffer keeps running in and out of the corn. Sometimes he barks and jumps up and down a lot. He really is silly.

Q. Is Scruffer your dog?

A. He's Gram's.

Q. What's he doing now?

A. He keeps jumping up and trying to bite Sally . . . stop that, Scruffer . . . that's a bad dog . . . you go home . . . you bad, Scruffer, I don't even like you anymore . . . Scruffer . . . SCRUFFER . . .

17

AW-A-A-A. (Cindy begins to cry and scream very loudly.)

Q. All right, I want you to let go of this and move one day forward in time. Now what are you doing, Cindy?

A. Sitting on the porch

Q. Can you tell me about what happened yesterday?

A. I hate Scruffer . . . someday I'm going to kill him. He is the worst dog in the whole world.

Q. What did that bad old Scruffer do?

A. He bit Sally and ripped open her head, and all her stuffin's came out . . . he wouldn't let go, and he pulled me over and made me scrape my face right here . . . see? Mommy and Gram and Uncle Bill looked all over the corn fields, and nobody can find Sally. I hate Scruffer so much.

Q. Where is old Scruffer right now?

A. I don't know . . . I'm staying on the porch to get away from him. I'm so glad we're going home tomorrow . . . there won't be any dogs there.

Q. You don't have a dog at home, then?

A. No . . . and I don't want any old dirty dogs, either. Mommy is going to get me another doll, but I want Sally. I had Sally from when I was a baby. (She begins to cry again.)

This was the end of the regression portion of the session. I gave Cindy strong suggestions to rise above her phobia, and to let go of the past. She was then awakened.

"That damn old dog. I'd forgotten all about that incident. Could I have blocked it out of my mind?"

"Probably, Cindy. . . . You mentioned that you knew you had been fearful of dogs since you were a teenager. Can you remember the earliest incident and tell me about it?"

"Sure. I was over at a friend's house. I was wearing one of those long, sash-type belts that were popular many years ago. Her dog, which was just a little cocker, grabbed it while we were sitting down at the table doing our homework. He pulled and wouldn't let go, and

I got scared and started to cry. Wow . . . I guess that was a *déjà vu* experience, wasn't it?"

"You've repressed the initial experience so long that it has grown out of proportion over the years. In a case like this, the knowledge could release you from your anxiety. Let's approach it carefully at first. You can start by looking at pictures of dogs in a magazine or book. Relax and fantasize yourself being in a situation with a dog and feeling comfortable. Then you might go to a pet store and watch the puppies in the window from afar. If you feel good about one experience, move on to another that brings you a little closer, until you are able to actually pet a dog without feeling uneasy."

A month later, we received the following note:

Thanks a million. It worked. I didn't even take it slow, for on the way home from the hypnosis session, I was in a shopping center that had a pet store. I watched the puppies in the window and was charmed by their antics. To make a long story short, I actually patted several of the larger dogs on the head that very afternoon. Since then, I've been in the environment of friends' dogs on several occasions without any negative feelings. I have no desire to own one myself, but I also have no fear, and I feel released.

Love,
Cindy

Lana Harley
Age: 56
Widow
Housewife
Problem: fear of heights

Lana was planning to participate in a cross-country bus tour with other widowed and retired people from her area. The highlights were to be Washington, D.C., and New York City. "How can I possibly enjoy these places I've always wanted to see, when I'm so afraid of heights that it almost makes me sick in the stomach just to think about it?" she asked. "I'll be waiting on the bus while the rest of the tour sees the Empire State Building and the Statue of Liberty," she sighed with a note of resignation.

The tour was beginning in a month, which didn't leave enough time to ensure the success of reprogramming techniques. I decided to use regressive hypnosis in an attempt to uncover the cause of Lana's phobia.

Hypnosis was induced, and she was instructed to go back to the origin of her present-day fear of heights.

Q. Can you speak up and tell me what you see and what you are doing at this time?
A. I'm at the fair with my beau.
Q. Can you tell me a little more about the fair and what you are doing?
A. We are just walking along looking at all the pretty lights and the people . . . they're all dressed up. We are standing by the merry-go-round, and the children are all so happy. Roger is laughing at one little boy who is hanging on to his horse so tightly his knuckles are white.
Q. What year is this?
A. Nineteen-twenty.
Q. Can you tell me what is happening now?
A. We're getting into a chair on the Ferris wheel ride. I told Roger that I hope my stomach is up to it, or he might regret talking me into such a folly. Oh, my goodness . . . we are up so high . . . we can see the whole fairgrounds and even the city, off, over there.
Q. Continue to relate what is transpiring.
A. We're just going round and round . . . the going up is all right, but the coming down makes my stomach feel funny. Roger thinks I'm very funny . . . he . . . oh . . . OH, NO . . . ! (Lana lurched forward in the chair, then slumped, and the verbal communication was ended.)

Q. All right, you have the power and ability to speak up and verbally talk to me, regardless of your environment. I want you to tell me what you are experiencing at this time.

A. Floating . . . I'm just floating . . . looking at Roger and myself lying there on the ground. People are running around. They put something over me, and they are carrying Roger off on a stretcher.

Q. How do you feel? Do you feel anything at all?

A. No . . . I don't feel anything, but I'm afraid . . . I think I might be dead.

Q. Can you tell me what happened on the Ferris wheel?

A. When we were at the top and just starting to come down, one side of the chair broke loose, and we fell out . . . I think that's what happened . . . everything seems so strange now.

Q. I want you to be relaxed now and at ease. You have left the physical body and are now in spirit. If you look around, I'm sure you will sense the presence of others there with you. They will help you.

A. Oh, yes . . . yes . . .

Q. Let's let go of this now; you are going to let go and come back to the present time, remaining in a deep hypnotic sleep . . . but on the count of three, you'll be back in the present time in Scottsdale, Arizona . . . remembering everything you experienced while in the past.

After Lana was awakened, we discussed the regression. "I've always felt that reincarnation was probable, but I've never been a big reader on the subject, and I'm certainly not that interested in mystical philosophy," she explained. "One interesting thing, though. I hate amusement parks and have never been on a Ferris wheel in my life. At least not this life," she added.

In this case, as with Cindy's, knowing the cause eliminated the effect. Lana rose above her fear of heights and went on to have a successful tour. She sent us a postcard from the Empire State Building.

Your past is affecting you. Some of the effects result from tangible experiences, as in the two cases I've just described, but others are quite subtle. Researchers are beginning to discover that, even from the limited perspective of your current lifetime, your present personality is being affected by an almost unlimited number of past experiences. For example:

1. The circumstances of your birth, including the physical environment, method of delivery, and the attitude of doctors, nurses, and your parents.
2. Your position within the family, whether you are the oldest, the youngest, or an only child.
3. The way you were treated during the first year of your life. For example, how did your parents respond to your cries for attention, or the lack or abundance of physical contact?
4. The relationship of family members to each other. For example, if your mother is more aggressive than your father, it will probably have affected the way you approach your career.

But your personality isn't the only thing being affected by your past. Even your physical reality is a result of the past. Following are two examples:

1. If you're allergic to milk, it could be because your ancestors weren't milk drinkers. It takes many generations for the human body to adapt to drinking cows' milk.
2. In the early 1960s, the DES babies were certainly a product of their mothers' past. Drugs taken during pregnancy resulted in a small percentage of their daughters developing cancer as teenagers.

For the most part, the past is an unseen influence. Few of us remember past incidents that result in fears and hangups today. One of my subjects was a workaholic whose intense drive was ruining his marriage. When I regressed him back to the cause, he reexperienced being nine years old and going through terrible traumas during fourth-grade recess. Because he was not well coordinated, he was always the last one chosen for sports activities. His "someday I'll show you" fantasies carried forward as an excessive drive for a successful career.

In the case of Cindy's fear of dogs, there is no doubt that regressive hypnosis released valid, traumatic memories that had been repressed since childhood. But what about Lana's accident? Was it a past-life memory of the Ferris wheel accident, or a psychodrama created as an excuse to let go of a phobia she was subconsciously ready to relinquish anyway? After fourteen years of investigation and having conducted thousands of past-life regressions, there is no way I can responsibly say that reincarnation is an absolute. Many believers who have listened to my words in public have been quite antagonized by my perspective. They demand to know why I'm not a total believer, since I have written books on the subject and devoted so much of my life to investigating the metaphysical world.

The answer is simple. You have to believe on the basis of faith, not facts, because the facts do not add up to an absolute. Upon investigating past-life regressions, I found individuals who existed just as the hypnotized subject described, and facts have been verified to the smallest detail, but that doesn't prove reincarnation. There is always the possibility that the subject was once exposed to this knowledge and has since forgotten. Maybe the subject drew the memory from someone's mind via extrasensory means, such as telepathy or electromagnetic waves. Another explanation is that we have the ability to tap the collective unconscious of all mankind. In regressions that are not verifiable, the information could be a self-created psychodrama that fits the psychological needs of the individual.

I am not relating this information to discredit the concept of reincarnation, but rather to be objective. I do believe reincarnation is valid. In *Past Lives, Future Loves,* I explained my belief that we are affected by events that transpired in times prior to our birth. This belief is based upon the experiences of years of research, obvious patterns, and too many coincidences to ignore. I realize this isn't proof, but faith. I call it "reincarnation," but as is explained in the previously mentioned book, I'm not sure how it works. I offer six primary possibilities beyond the accepted belief system that we live, die, and are reborn into a new life to work out the karma from the past.

They are: 1. The Creator Concept; 2. The Oversoul Concept; 3. The Total Illusion Concept; 4. The Energy Immortality Concept; 5. The Advanced Souls Return Concept; and 6. The Schoolhouse Concept. Without going into detail about these concepts, I will say that it seems most likely that we are somehow linked to people who have lived before us by a spiritual genetic lineage. I'm not speaking of our genetic ancestors, but of other individuals who existed on our wavelength or frequency. This results in an influence that can span centuries. Actually, this becomes an intellectual exercise in semantics, for if the people from history are an influence, then what is the difference if they were us or not? The result is the same.

Although we can't prove reincarnation, I can provide evidence of patterns that exist and remain constant, regardless of how large a group is or in what geographical area they live. For example, when a group of people are regressed to their first life on Earth, the following patterns emerge: 1. about 55% of the group will have strong impressions of a primitive lifetime; 2. another 10% will see themselves in an environment of an advanced early civilization, such as Atlantis or Lemuria; 3. approximately 10% experience an environment in which they are crossing over from nonphysical to physical, requiring no material sustenance;

4. and 5. the remaining individuals are usually divided between experiencing Earth arrival either via extraterrestrial means, or as "light forms" that are transferred into physical forms. For an entire year of touring, I did not mention anything about what to expect in this regression. It was only after all of the five possible first incarnations were introduced by participants who experienced them and the regression was concluded that I asked for verification by a show of hands. Phoenix, Los Angeles, San Francisco, Portland, Seattle, Atlanta, Houston, Dallas, New York City, and Las Vegas—the pattern remained constant within a few percentage points.

Other patterns that remain constant through several lifetimes relate to current talents or interests. For example, a "natural-born salesman" might perceive a past life as a merchant in an Arabian desert caravan 200 years ago. The karate enthusiast might have experienced a past lifetime as a Naja warrior in feudal Japan.

In many cases, we have been able to substantiate facts and minor details to such a degree that I question the possibility of psychodrama. But there is another possibility that should be considered. That is the power of our mind to draw knowledge from the past as it becomes important to us. As you become more and more interested in karate, your desire to excel and your interest create a tie to what has happened in the past. Perhaps there was a Naja warrior who existed on your frequency, and his energy remains available. Thus, you begin to draw upon his knowledge and accelerate your own advancement. I have seen numerous cases in which artists, writers, and musicians seem to be linked to the past in this way. Career similarities are found in a high percentage of regressions.

In conclusion, the past is an unseen influence. Past lives cannot be proven to be one of the influences, but evidence supports the concept that we mentally tap sources of knowledge to which we have never been consciously exposed in our current life. We have the ability to draw upon the knowledge of those who have lived before us.

Chapter 3

UNRECOGNIZED ALTERED STATES

If you're wide awake and fully alert, you are functioning in a "beta" brain-wave level. This is a frequency of mind activity that is measurable on an EEG machine; if converted to sound, it is a clicking of about 850 beats per minute in the mid-beta range. When a conditioned subject goes into hypnosis or meditation, he reduces the frequency of mental activity to that of his natural depth. For most people, that would be a clicking of about 140 beats per minute. Any level of alpha, or deeper, is an altered state of consciousness.

Brain researchers and medical practitioners have divided the brain into four levels of cycles-per-second activity:

1. *BETA:*
   Full consciousness
2. *ALPHA:*
   ————————————————————⌐
   Crossing over into sleep |
   Awakening in A.M.   ↓
   Hypnosis   Altered State
   Meditation
3. *THETA:*
   Early stages of sleep
   Deep hypnosis
   Deep meditation
4. *DELTA:*
   Full to deep sleep

Everyone goes into an altered state at least twice daily—upon going to sleep you slow down from beta to delta, and upon awakening you return. Thus, everyone is familiar with these levels. It is important to realize that there is no one special mental category for hypnosis and another one for meditation. These are only varying levels of an altered state of consciousness. For most people, hypnosis is identical to the time just before opening your eyes in the morning. Your conscious mind is connected, you hear all sounds in the room, but you aren't yet fully conscious.

Purposeful self-hypnosis and meditation create desirable altered states that can be used for programming or enlightenment, but there are many other situations that can result in an altered state of consciousness. Problems can result when the altered state isn't recognized. Some people are simply more susceptible to trance levels than others. Stage hypnotists can quickly find the somnambulists in their audience by conducting a group hypnosis session that shows the degree of body relaxation, the amount of eye movement, and the responsiveness to various suggestions among the participants. The hypnotist then chooses somnambulists to perform in the show.

During a stage show, the hypnotist might tell a male participant from the audience that he will perform a perfectly beautiful hula dance. The subject responds accordingly, for he has chosen to accept the hypnotist's belief that he can do the hula. The subject had previously seen a hula dance on TV, in a movie, or in person, so the knowledge of how to do it was locked in the memory bank of his subconscious. The suggestion expanded his belief system so that he believed he could do the dance; thus, he could.

Most people are not capable of this deep-level trance, but at least 25% come close to it. Everyone, with the exception of the mentally deranged, is capable of attaining some degree of altered state of consciousness. My own experience in hypnotizing thousands of people results in the conclusion that over 90% are capable of mid-range to medium-deep hypnosis. You need only achieve a light alpha state to reprogram your subconscious mind with positive suggestions.

So what causes the fully conscious individual to go into an altered state? In hypnosis, it is usually body relaxation and a carefully patterned voice roll. The hypnotist speaks with a regular beat, as if matching his words to a metronome, which he also may use. Some hypnotists use a brain-wave synchronizer or strobe light in combination with their verbal pattern to achieve the same results. I have hypnotized as many as 1,000 people at a time using this technique, and virtually everyone achieved some degree of trance. The majority of the audience needed my full six-minute induction to attain the altered state of consciousness, but most of the somnambulists in the group were in a deep state within a minute or two.

The Potentials

Any repetitive sound or motion can potentially alter a somnambulist's consciousness very quickly. Watching television often creates an altered state of consciousness, because the television screen, while appearing static, actually flickers. If your memory lapses while watching television, you may be a somnambulist. Other trance devices may be as inconspicuous as the sound of a grandfather clock ticking in a quiet room, or as disconcerting as the flash of a strobe light in a discothèque. The somnambulist is vulnerable to most rhythmic, sustained patterns of sound or light.

It isn't only the somnambulist who is affected. I use this type as an example because the results are more immediate and dramatic, but everyone is affected to some degree. This will vary according to an individual's natural trance ability and the conditions that influence the achievement of an altered state, such as the temperature of the room, the time of day, or the subject's degree of fatigue.

Having observed people in strobe-light discothèques, I believe that the majority have had their consciousness

This was perceived by the subconscious minds of the people in the audience, while their conscious minds were totally unaware. The subconscious is easily programmed, and the result was higher sales at the snack stand. The government outlawed this form of subliminal advertising, but there are many other subtle ways to program a viewer hypnotically.

One way is to make sure the viewer is in a trance before seeing the commercial. This is easily accomplished by flickering the light on the TV screen in a rhythmic pattern. There are normally 24 frames per second, or 1,440 frames per minute, in full animation. By inserting a blank frame every 36 frames for three minutes before the commercial, Sugar Zappies are hitting the viewer with a full 40-beats-per-minute induction. This is the perfect pulsation for hypnosis, yet the viewer would consciously perceive only the seemingly smooth action of the cartoons.

At the commercial break, though, the makers of Sugar Zappies have the viewer in their sugar-coated hands: "Tell your mom you won't settle for anything but Sugar Zappies for a healthy breakfast. You want Sugar Zappies tomorrow morning!" the announcer hypnotically commands. The hypnotized child hears, believes, and responds according to subliminal programming. How many of you have seen that glassy-eyed look on your children's faces? Or, while watching television yourself, how many of you have not heard someone asking a question because you were so absorbed? Absorbed?

Although there are laws against subliminal programming, this kind of mental manipulation of the public has thus far escaped legal action. Public awareness is the first step toward protection, followed by a strong law against any form of subliminal audio or video modification. Random monitoring should follow, with severe consequences for violators. As a known hypnotist, I have been contacted on more than one occasion by representatives of politicians, asking me to actually record the voice-over for their commercials "with that convincing technique"!

Unrecognized altered states aren't always created by external situations. You can unwittingly create them yourself. For example, the easy rhythm, the repetitive movement, and the sound of running in a quiet environment are conducive to an altered state of consciousness. I am a runner, and although I rarely went into a trance when I first began running, once I got past the self-critical phase to where I could run five to ten miles without effort, I found that I was slipping into a trance after about two miles. My eyes were open, I was totally aware of my surroundings, and ideas and creative concepts poured into my consciousness the same way they do when I purposely seek knowledge in self-hypnosis.

Los Angeles reality therapist Dr. William Glasser has been working with runners in an attempt to understand their "highs." He explores the phenomenon in his book *Positive Addiction*. According to Glasser, runners who have developed their long-distance abilities become literally addicted to their sport, and some of them experience withdrawal symptoms if they can't run or are forced to quit for a while due to an injury.

Why? Because they have developed, along with their running abilities, an addiction to an internally manufactured opiate called enkephaline. Produced in the brain, enkephaline's chemical composition resembles that of heroin, as does its effect. Production and release of the chemical are triggered by a shift from left-brain activity to right-brain activity, which amounts to an alteration of one's state of consciousness.

Not all runners feel they get "high" when they run. Some claim little effect, while others place it on a level of spiritual transformation. I'm a mid-range hypnosis subject, and I'd place my runner's "high" about mid-range, as well. I believe that testing would prove somnambulist runners experience the most extreme "highs."

This understanding also explains another phenomenon that a few runners have experienced: astral projection while running. This is usually described as follows: "All of a sudden I seemed to rise above myself, watching myself run along the road." After years of working with astral projection, Trenna and I are convinced that no one consciously projects, even if he thinks he does. There is always something, such as deep breathing prior to the experience, that alters consciousness.

Running can cause an altered state, and I suspect that easy walking can do the same thing. I believe that there are many frequencies of time and space. We could be living in one frequency, while another simultaneous reality is only a frequency away—like radio stations on a dial, you tune in to one at a time. We know that there are sounds beyond our hearing range, and if an object vibrates fast enough, it disappears from our vision. Now, project this oversimplified theory into a hypothetical situation in which a hunter is walking through the woods in an altered state of consciousness. This mental state allows him unknowingly to tune in two stations at one time, and he sees Bigfoot!

This information may also explain why so many responsible people have sighted UFOs that others haven't seen. A high percentage of the sightings have occurred while people are driving on lonely roads at night. The yellow line goes by, flicking hypnotically, and the driver, with no other traffic or distractions to disturb him, drifts into a deep altered state of consciousness with his eyes wide open. Thus, he sees something that exists in another frequency. Some researchers believe UFOs can switch frequencies at will. This explains why they can disappear before the eyes of observers or vanish from a radar screen.

Have you ever been driving and suddenly realized that you can't recall traversing the last several miles? "How did I get here already . . . ? I don't even recall passing Smith Junction." An altered state may be the explanation, and it should alert you to future driving situations. The flicking yellow line is one consideration. Windshield wipers clicking back and forth at approximately 40 beats per minute are potentially even more dangerous. Few somnambulists can resist the lulling effect, and everyone else will be somewhat affected.

A row of trees on the east or west side of the road

can also create an altered state of consciousness. When the sun is rising above or setting behind those trees, an intense flickering effect is created that affects all those driving down the road. Highway authorities should check for this potential hazard along any stretch of road that has been the location of an excessive number of one-car accidents.

While explaining these situations in a seminar, I noticed the reaction of a woman in the front row, Marcia Miller, an attorney. The seminar had included several group hypnosis experiences, so I was aware that Marcia was one of the deepest-level somnambulists attending. She raised her hand.

"Can I share my own experience to verify your statements?" she asked. "I was driving a Winnebago motor home cross-country a few months ago. It was on cruise control, and I simply got up out of the driver's seat while the vehicle was still moving and went to the rear to use the bathroom. Naturally, it went crashing off the road, and, thank goodness, neither I nor it was badly hurt. Until now, I couldn't understand how I did it."

Beth, a young Indian girl from the Navajo reservation, was another somnambulist in the group. She showed us her badly scarred arm. She had sustained her injury in an accident in which she was driving. Without realizing what had happened, she suddenly had found herself upside down in the car. There had been no alcohol or excessive speed involved.

Although I've used somnambulists to illustrate what can result from being in unrecognized altered states, everyone is affected to some degree by these situations. Also, people who deliberately spend time in an altered state of consciousness, such as running or self-hypnosis, run an additional risk: they may never come back to full beta consciousness. They may stay more or less permanently in right-brain function, which is characterized by a relaxed personality, creative problem solving, and intuitive, rather than deductive, perception abilities.

A friend of mine is a dentist, and he became involved in meditation as an effective way of coping with the stress in his life. He used meditation techniques for forty minutes every morning and every evening. After a couple of years, his wife complained that he was becoming dull, and he agreed that he didn't seem to have as much to say to people as he did in the past. A medical friend checked him on an EEG machine and found that he was in an alpha state when apparently wide awake.

If you wish to avoid a constant alpha state of mind, be aware of all the situations described in this chapter. If you feel yourself slipping into a trance when it isn't appropriate, simply count yourself awake: "On the count of five I will be wide awake." Always do this after a long run or during a tedious drive—unless, of course, you'd rather stay in alpha all the time and remain mellow, relaxed, and creative.

I used to work with my own self-hypnosis tapes once or twice a day for years without permanently altering my waking consciousness, because the tapes are short and fully awaken you with a "one-two-three-four-five, wide awake" command. But when I became a conditioned distance runner, I drifted into an altered state for an hour or two at a time while running and never awakened myself afterward. Running began to take the place of all but one goal-programming hypnosis session a day. I realized that I was internalizing more than ever before and was remaining in light alpha. Many of my business, social, and personal encounters served as telling examples to those close to me. I was quieter, more withdrawn, yet more creative and productive than I was before taking up running.

The question was: Did I want to do something about it? The answer was no. Programming or an after-run technique—such as sticking my head under the faucet and counting up—would cause a return to full consciousness. Light alpha is less stressful and more desirable to me, and it doesn't seem to have any detrimental effects. I can judge from my martial arts reaction timing that I am as physically alert as ever. I teach other people how to recognize immediately any form of

35

external manipulation, so I'm not concerned about being negatively programmed as a result of being in a suggestible state. In reality, combining the alpha brain-wave level with the philosophy I communicate results in a more mellow life for me, but I do not advocate this for everyone. All individuals experience reality differently. The high-powered business executive might cease to be as effective in a more relaxed mental state. The somnambulist might slip too deeply into an altered state, resulting in slowed reaction time or blanking out, as I discussed previously. Deciding what's best for you must be a personal exploration and decision.

Chapter 4

CUMULATIVE EFFECTS

The purpose of this chapter is to increase your awareness of one aspect of your diet: the cumulative effects of the chemicals, additives, preservatives, and trace elements you inhale or ingest. They are a primary unseen influence. To attain freedom from negative influences, you must achieve optimum health, which is your natural state when you aren't polluting your system with all the aforementioned items. There is no single book or individual authority that covers all cumulative effects. You can't trust the A.M.A. or the government to guide you. Giant food manufacturers are responsible for a criminal amount of irresponsible and misleading dietary information which is presented as nutritional wisdom. The multibillion-dollar drug industry is the self-serving power that influences the medical industry, often offering side effects and degenerative consequences exceeding the original problem. There is little monetary profit in helping people to keep their bodies healthy enough to fight and win their medical battles. Thus, of the 454,464 doctors in this country, only 769 specialize in preventive medicine (A.M.A. 1979 figures). And most of these physicians just give preventive vaccinations.

A many-volumed set of books could be written on the subject of this chapter alone, but to inspire you to become your own researcher, I will offer some typical examples of the misinformation with which we are currently being deluged.

"So I drink a few cans of diet cola a day. . . . There certainly isn't enough saccharin in a can to worry about. The authorities just made them put that dumb warning label on it. It doesn't mean anything."

"I've smoked cigarettes for twelve years, and I haven't gotten lung cancer or emphysema yet."

These are typical reactions that I've heard hundreds of times. People rationalize their lack of common sense and self-control in strange ways.

We have to realize that trace amounts over ten or twenty years accumulate into substantial amounts, and the result is degenerative disease. Until you understand and respect healthy life-style principles, you can expect to become less healthy as you grow older.

Margarine is a good example of the undesirable results of processing food. I'll begin with the hydrogenation process that is used in manufacturing margarine. Hydrogenation is the chemical procedure by which liquid oil is converted into solid margarine.

After heating oil in a pressurized container, hydrogen gas is pumped through the oil in the presence of nickel, a catalyst agent. Nickel causes hydrogen and carbon to pick up extra bonds of hydrogen; that's what makes the liquid oil harden into solid margarine.

One flaw in this process is that there is no way to reclaim all the nickel, so every time you eat margarine you ingest trace amounts of nickel, as well. What are the cumulative effects of nickel? For one, nickel is a suspected carcinogen (cancer-producing substance), and some health specialists feel it interferes with the nervous system, weakening muscular power.

An even more important flaw in hydrogenation is the result of the process itself. Hydrogenation succeeds not only in clogging up liquid oil, but it also clogs up your arteries.

The next consideration is the polyunsaturates used in many margarines and oils. Polyunsaturates, which are basically fats that become liquid at room temperature, are advertised and promoted as a great health benefit. In actuality, it is a merchandising gimmick for a substance that is probably causing far more harm than good. If your diet is high in polyunsaturates, you are depleting the vitamin E in your body; without E, red blood cells can be destroyed. There is evidence that polyunsaturates increase blood pressure, and a plastic surgeon reported that 78% of his patients eating high-polyunsaturated diets showed signs of premature aging. In a Mayo Clinic study, it was found that high concentrations of polyunsaturated fats were discovered in the blood and diseased tissue of breast-cancer patients. A Los Angeles veterans' hospital study showed that patients fed a high-polyunsaturated diet developed 60% more cancers than a control group.

When a polyunsaturated fat is heated, as in a frying pan, it becomes far more dangerous, as extensive laboratory tests have well proven. The evidence of the dangers continues to be gathered, while the advertising continues to sell a lot of profitable products to a naïve public.

"Okay, okay, so maybe I should give up margarine, and I'll skip products with polyunsaturates, but I sure can't eat butter because of the cholesterol. What do they expect me to do?"

Cholesterol. The very word strikes fear in the hearts of all who are concerned about heart disease, yet major medical names are speaking out against this scare, which they consider to be one of the biggest blunders ever committed by the medical establishment. By adhering to the cholesterol theory, they have boxed themselves into a corner and can't change positions without losing face. Yet, the most recent evidence indicates that those who have the most to lose by the public's consumption of cholesterol are the food manufacturers marketing margarines and egg substitutes.

Advertising and public relations firms and some medical clinics would have you believe that if a little cholesterol is bad, then more is worse. In reality, cholesterol is absolutely essential to life. It is the molecular base from which adrenaline hormones, sex hormones, vitamin D, and bile acids are formed. It is part of the membrane that surrounds all the cells in your body. It is a protective covering of the nerve fibers, and it makes up part of the brain. Cholesterol is absolutely essential to normal growth, longevity, and resistance to infection.

It is true that you must be concerned by the amount of cholesterol in your blood, but that doesn't necessarily relate to the amount in your diet. Most of the cholesterol in your blood is manufactured by your own body. Only 20% to 30% comes from the food you eat. If you consume an excess of cholesterol, your body will manufacture less. If you don't eat enough cholesterol, your own liver and intestines will manufacture more to regulate the proper amount.

There are extensive medical reports and research studies to substantiate the fact that the relationship between cholesterol and heart disease is so tenuous as to be almost mythical. Laymen can read much more detailed evidence in the books of Dr. Robert Atkins, Dr. Richard Passwater, and many others.

The real dietary culprits in heart disease and elevated triglyceride levels are sugar and refined carbohydrates, and there have already been several books written on this subject.

Let's examine some additional food items. It seems that if we are not being sold a bill of goods, we're often being sold food that is not fit for human consumption.

Carrots

Lead is a primary pollutant released into the atmosphere from the exhaust fumes of automobiles. A commercial truck farm located along a major roadway was slowly contaminated over the years by the pollutants being absorbed into the soil of the fields. The pollutants, in turn, were absorbed by the fruits and vegetables grown there. A test done on a carrot crop disclosed that a deadly amount of lead in the carrots had resulted in the poisoning of many people. Lead has a degenerative effect on the central nervous system, and even in small amounts it can damage the liver, kidneys, heart, and other body organs.

It is important to do everything possible to obtain poison-free produce. Buy it directly from the grower, grow your own, or at least question your food store about its produce suppliers.

Ice Cream

At one time, ice cream was made of whole eggs, milk, and honey, and it was a healthful treat. Today it has become a mass-produced synthetic, with 1,200 different chemicals, emulsifiers, bactericides, neutralizers, and artificial flavors and colors that are legally allowed in the manufacture of the product. Ice cream manufacturers are not required to list the additives that go into their products, and there are no federal regulations limiting the amount of harmful bacteria, for individual states have been allowed to set their own limits. Some impressive tests, including one conducted by *Consumer Reports,* have found excessive bacteria counts, and even fecal streptococci counts, in many samples.

Yet, the government-approved chemicals that are allowed as ingredients are the most shocking. Documented analysis has shown the common use of the following:

- *Butyraldehyde:* creates a nutty flavor and is a common ingredient in rubber cement.
- *Diethylene glycol:* used as an emulsifier substitute for eggs. This chemical is also used in paint remover and antifreeze.
- *Ethyl acetate:* creates a pineapple flavor and is also used as a leather and textile cleaner. The

vapors of this chemical have been known to cause severe lung, liver, and heart damage.
- *Piperonal:* replaces vanilla and is a chemical used to kill lice.
- *Aldehyde C17:* flavors cherry ice cream and is an inflammable liquid used in aniline dyes, plastic, and rubber.
- *Benzyl acetate:* flavors strawberry ice cream and is a nitrate solvent.

And there are many, many more chemicals used in ice cream that are just as appetizing.

Sprayed Fruits and Vegetables

Agribusiness covers potential losses by doing everything in its power to ensure high yields. Insects potentially threaten farmers' profits, so they automatically spray the crops with malathion, parathion, and countless other pesticides. Little does it matter that many chemicals may slowly weaken and destroy the lives of the millions of people who ingest them into their systems.

If you are eating fruits and vegetables purchased at the supermarket, you must peel or wash them much more carefully than you are presently doing. They must be washed in warm water by brushing with soap or mild detergent, and then rinsed many times to remove all traces of soap. Some people use diluted hydrolic acid to remove the surface contaminants. Nothing can remove those absorbed from the soil.

These sprays and waxes are oil soluble, and a quick wash in cold water is worthless. Not everyone is aware that those "super-shiny" apples and other fruits and vegetables in the supermarket are waxed. If you doubt it, run your fingernail along the surface and watch it peel away. Then yell at the produce manager. The wax is used to retard water loss; thus, the shelf life of the produce is extended. Of course, this process seals in whatever residue of pesticide, dye, or gas may remain on the produce.

Sesame Seeds

Please realize that I am not writing about a few specific foods that should concern you. I am using random examples of foods to exemplify the concern you should have for everything that enters your mouth. Sesame seeds certainly seem harmless enough, right? If they are non-chemically hulled, sesame is a very high-quality protein, containing all of the essential amino acids needed by the body for growth, maintenance, and reproduction. Sesame's protein content of 20% exceeds that of beef (18%), eggs (13%), and whole milk (3.5%). It also contains lecithin for the heart vessels and is a highly digestible source of essential fatty acids and several B vitamins. It is well endowed with inositol, choline, and thiamine. It provides vitamin E, which strengthens the heart, blood vessels, and nerves; it also offers a higher potassium content than bananas. Several additional pages could be spent talking about the benefits of sesame, for it is one of the most perfect foods available to us—if correctly processed.

The problem begins with unhulled sesame seeds. In its unhulled state, as you will find it 99% of the time, sesame should not be eaten. The hull contains a toxic form of calcium oxalate that is unfit for human consumption. It robs the body of stored calcium, for one thing. And for another, eating foods high in calcium oxalate can result in urinary infections, kidney stones, digestive upsets, diarrhea, cardiovascular disorders, arthritis, gout, allergic reactions, and tooth decay.

And most sesame is not only unhulled; it's also unclean. Sesame grows in hot climates where farmers pick it by hand. The bacteria that grow on the seeds are not removable by washing.

Once it's hulled and cleaned by mechanical means, sesame will do more for you than most other foods. The key phrase is "mechanical means." Most sesame manufacturers strip the hulls with chemical processors and corrosive chemicals, simply substituting one evil for another, but there is one manufacturer that strips by mechanical means. Check with any health-food store for its sources.

Sesame seeds, by the way, are not the only source of calcium oxalate. Some other foods that contain this toxic substance are spinach, Swiss chard, rhubarb, beet greens, and chocolate. According to a recent U.S.D.A. report, the oxalate content of natural sesame seeds is ten times that of the other foods mentioned above.

Chicken

Forty years ago, it took farmers three to four months and five pounds of natural feed to produce one pound of chicken meat. Today, it takes nine weeks and two and a half pounds of "doctored feed" to achieve the same results. The breeders are experimenting with techniques to do it with two pounds of feed. Today, 90% of all chickens eat arsanilic acid, an arsenic substance which is mixed into the feed as a growth stimulant. Since the substance is toxic to humans, no one would consider feeding it to anyone. It's much more profitable to feed it to the chickens we eat.

To help chickens resist disease before they make it to the supermarket, they are automatically given antibiotics. Naturally, we ingest the same antibiotics when we eat the chicken. The F.D.A. also permits breeders to dip the carcasses into an antibiotic solution which increases the shelf life of the chicken, while leaving you with a residue that may reduce your own health.

Many other drugs and additives are often added to poultry feed. The use of tranquilizers to ease the tensions of scratching in a tiny cage instead of a barnyard, and the use of aspirin to fatten chickens and to ease their suffering from crowded environments are commonly accepted practices. Hormones are used to fatten the birds and tenderize the meat.

Virtually all tests of poultry have found the birds to

be contaminated with pesticide residue. In one case, the U.S.D.A. tested 2,000 samples from every federally inspected plant in this country and had the same results.

There are many other poultry processes that are enough to turn the stomachs of those exposed to this information for the first time. One of the processes begins while the chicken is still alive, just before it is killed. A hyaluronidase enzyme, mixed with sage, garlic, and nutmeg, is injected into the chicken, and the mixture spreads quickly through the bird before it dies. The real purpose is to deodorize and hide the cooking odors created by the chemicals and other adulterating processes that have been used in readying the chicken for your table.

The bottom line is that these processes often cause cancer in the chickens, and the breeders gamble on getting the birds to market before they contract the disease. They aren't always successful. Representatives of the poultry industry estimate that they must destroy $150,000,000 worth of cancerous chickens annually. If that isn't frightening enough, a U.S. government report revealed that a high percentage of the marketed chickens have leukosis—chicken cancer. The tumors are cut out, and what remains of the bird is sold as chicken parts in your grocery store or eating establishment.

I am not attempting to build a case for practicing vegetarianism, but I *am* issuing a loud warning to seek reputable suppliers; they do exist, but you will pay more. Don't take anyone's word for how the poultry and livestock are raised. Go see for yourself.

If you are interested in vegetarianism, your own investigation of the meat industry may be the push you need to make the step. In addition to easier assurance of healthful meals, vegetarianism has other advantages. In keeping with the studies of Dr. Irving Fisher of Yale University, Trenna and I found a vegetarian diet provided us with more stamina. As we are both dedicated racing runners, this was very important and readily demonstrable. Fisher put meat eaters and vegetarians through a series of endurance tests which proved vegetarians could outperform their carnivorous opponents.

Cheese and Antidepressants

The cumulative effects of drugs should be of great concern to anyone using them. There were 59,600,000 prescriptions issued for Valium in 1978 alone. That means between 15% and 20% of the people in this country live with stress that is too great for them to handle on their own. The drug temporarily relaxes them, but if they don't reduce the stress, they'll be on antidepressants forever. Often, the stress is the result of improper diet, or a combination of diet and personal problems.

Food and drug combinations can create totally new problems, because some nontoxic foods become toxic under certain conditions. For example, cheese contains amines (a toxic substance) that are normally detoxified in your body by monoamine oxidase. However, when you take some antidepressants with cheese, the drug inhibits the detoxification process. Some of the symptoms of these near-lethal combinations are nausea, achiness, depression, and irritability.

Aluminum

America's love affair with aluminum has potentially disastrous consequences. We cook in aluminum pans, use the foil in food preparation and storage, and buy TV dinners and other ready-to-use meals which are packaged in it. Soda pop comes in aluminum cans. Much of our drinking water is treated with alum, which leaves an aluminum trace in the water. Aluminum compounds are in most deodorants that you roll or spray directly onto your skin. Antacid tablets are loaded with it, and it is in many baking powders.

Aluminum remains stable when cold; however, when it is warm, as in a soft-drink can or when used in food preparation, aluminum will leach into the food. Current medical evidence documents how an excess of this element in the body can lead to dangerously degenerative effects. Senility, a state of mind ranging from being forgetful to forgetting everything you know, is one of the primary dangers. There are many more.

Additives

"BHT, a preservative, is added."

"Disodium inosinate and disodium guanylate are added as flavor enhancers."

The next time you read such claims—or any of the hundreds of variations—on the labels of the packaged food you buy, realize that the average person eating supermarket products is ingesting five pounds of additives per year.

There are over 1,300 food additives currently approved for use as colors, flavors, preservatives, thickeners, and other food-controlling properties. The continuing discoveries of apparent connections linking certain additives with cancer and hyperactivity have even a U.S. Senate Select Committee suggesting that "there is justifiable cause to seek to reduce additive consumption to the greatest degree possible."

Protein

New research, long-term studies, and testing equipment are constantly updating our knowledge of nutrition. Changes in recommendations are assured, but one of the primary problems is the power of the special-interest groups to play down this information or override it with extensive advertising.

The beef industry is a perfect example, spending millions of dollars to convey misleading information regarding the need in human diet of abundant protein for good health. The facts no longer support this concept, and as a result, the United Nations' World Health Organization has lowered the daily recommendation for protein from 120 grams to only 46 grams. The average American consumes 100 grams daily, with many extensive meat eaters continuing to consume protein in quantities of over 200 grams daily.

So why is this really important? Because it is a known medical fact that, on the average, an adult ingesting over 90 grams of protein daily is likely to be losing bone calcium at an alarming rate, leading to osteoporosis, provided his phosphorus intake is high. In addition, anyone eating liberal amounts of meat, fish, milk, eggs, legumes, or grains is sure to be consuming an excess of phosphorus.

There are many studies to support these facts. Researchers at the University of Wisconsin found that young men consuming 140 grams of protein daily were losing bone calcium at a rate which, if continued, would leave them with no bones at all by their early fifties. Every single participant in this test experienced rapid bone deterioration. Women need less protein than men, so deterioration will start at a lower daily gram intake.

The Creighton University School of Medicine conducted major calcium-balance studies on a large group of average women between thirty-five and forty-five years old. All were eating their normal diet, and on the average they were losing calcium at a rate of almost 2% of their total bone calcium yearly. Only 10% of the group were maintaining a calcium balance. This is documented evidence of devastating bone losses than can be projected to include the majority of the population of this country. The result: premature, "brittle" old age and degenerative disease. The increasing appearance of calcium-dependent atherosclerosis and arthritis at younger ages tends to support this premise. Pyorrhea and related teeth and gum problems also relate to a calcium-leaching condition.

In the United States, the primary protein authority is the Food and Nutrition Board of the National Research Council. The board now recommends .4 grams of protein daily per pound of adult body weight if your diet is based upon animal protein (66 grams for a 165-pound man; 51 grams for a 128-pound woman). If your diet is based primarily on plant protein, these

48

figures are increased greatly. Any physical or mental stress situation automatically increases your requirements and safe tolerance levels. An athlete, for instance, is experiencing unusual high bone stress, so he needs more protein.

Regardless of which set of figures you accept—those of the World Health Organization or the National Research Council—they are very low compared to the average protein intake, and they are a long, long way from what the meat industry would have you believe.

The National Cancer Institute conducted a cancer study of Japanese living in Hawaii. Some Japanese families maintained their native Oriental diet of fish, vegetables, and rice, while others adopted an American diet of meat and refined carbohydrates. The Institute said that in this test meat eating was the number one factor in the incidence of cancer.

The University of California conducted a large research project with Seventh Day Adventists, concluding that they contracted 40% to 60% less cancer than the average American due to the fact that most were vegetarian. It appears that the real problem with excessive protein intake boils down to excessive meat consumption.

"You are what you eat." Or maybe a better way to phrase it would be: "You will become in the future what you are eating now." Junk food equals a junky body. Healthy food equals a healthy body. The irony is that although it is the cumulative effects of food and food processes that so often create illness, it is also food which can return you to health.

Chapter 5

THE BODY/MIND CONNECTION

The United States ranks 89th in the world in life expectancy, and the only reason we're able to maintain that dubious honor is because of our excellent medical technology. Obviously, we are doing something very wrong, and it is time to make some changes.

An individual is ripe for change when he awakens one day to the fact that he isn't immortal—his diet and life-style have failed. All too often this comes as the result of health problems, for most of us are conditioned to respond to fear and pain, instead of foresight.

It used to be the contagious diseases such as tuberculosis, smallpox, and diphtheria that were the widespread killers. Today, we have all but conquered these ailments, only to replace them by a rising tide of chronic and degenerative conditions such as heart disease, cancer, cirrhosis of the liver, and diabetes. The situation would be bad enough if these conditions were present only in the aged, but the statistics prove that alarming numbers of younger persons are also being afflicted.

In the last ten years, the percentage of persons under seventeen years of age who are limited in their activities due to a chronic health condition has nearly doubled. The death rates for persons fifteen to twenty-four years old are increasing at an alarming rate. According to the 1977 Vital Statistics Reports, during the twelve-month period from July, 1976, to July, 1977, there was a 9.1% increase in the rate of deaths of people fifteen years old to twenty-four years old.

We are in the midst of an epidemic of chronic and degenerative diseases affecting all ages, and the two basic reasons are our diet and life-style. Even accidents, suicides, and alcohol/drug-related casualties can often be related to dietary sources that cause stress or alter body chemistry.

In *Past Lives, Future Loves,* I wrote about the case history of a metaphysical examination in which Trenna and I explored many interesting unseen influences that were affecting a troubled friend. One of his primary problems was hypoglycemia—low blood sugar. That chapter generated an avalanche of mail from people who had experienced similar situations.

Obviously, there is no way to cover as broad a subject as physical health in one chapter; therefore, I am going to use hypoglycemia as an example. I consider it the most widespread negative physical influence in our country and the primary factor in relationship problems. The chances are 50–50 that you already have it. If you're eating the standard American diet, you are rapidly moving toward this low-blood-sugar condition. It was the number one unseen influence, statistically, in all of the case histories Trenna and I have investigated.

I'm not a doctor, but I've had medical people come to me to ask about hypoglycemia. The head nurse of one hospital explained she could not find anything in medical books about it, but she was convinced that she and her husband were afflicted. After reading a magazine article I'd written, a local doctor asked me for all the additional information I could provide.

The reason there isn't more information on this widespread affliction is that it is a recent mass-degenerative disease. It isn't caused by germs; rather, it is a creation of our own desire for sweet and convenient foods. It results primarily from the cumulative effects of eating refined sugars and flours, which have become

51

increasingly available over the last forty years. In the entire known history of the world, man has never ingested a diet similar to that of our current generation. Affluence and advanced technology have resulted in tasty poisons for a human body genetically conditioned to whole, natural foods.

Eric and Ellen Fowler were on the verge of a divorce due to Eric's depressions and mood swings, which ranged from withdrawal to rages over trivial matters. His sex drive had dwindled to a merely occasional interest, and only if Ellen initiated it, and his only after-work "activity" consisted solely of watching television. "I don't have the energy to do anything else," he stated.

Eric was thirty-two and a successful architect. Two years earlier, none of these symptoms had existed. In fact, Ellen often jokingly called him "hyper," because he often worked on many home activities at once. A six-hour Glucose Tolerance Test confirmed that Eric had low blood sugar. The doctor who diagnosed his condition offered little practical advice on how to combat it, so Eric did his own research and improved his life-style by incorporating the Paavo Airola diet with a daily exercise program of running. Within a few weeks, all the symptoms were gone, and he felt better than he could ever remember. "I used to drink an excess of coffee or cola and eat sweets to help make my work deadlines," he explained. "Between the stress and the excess of sugar and caffeine, I'm sure I accelerated the disease."

Authorities on hypoglycemia agree that between 40% and 50% of the population of the United States are afflicted to some degree, and that 25% are severely affected, although most sufferers don't recognize the real problem.

Hypoglycemia is a condition in which the body removes glucose (sugar) from the blood faster than it replaces it. Quickly assimilated carbohydrates, such as alcohol, candy, cola, or sugar products, send the victim's blood sugar soaring, only to have it drop to an abnormal low a few hours later. The body's release

52

of adrenaline to correct the low-sugar situation causes the peculiar mental and emotional responses.

The Wall Street Journal ran a story linking low blood sugar to crimes including assaults, sexual offenses, and murders without motives.

An Ohio probation officer puts hypoglycemic offenders on a high-protein diet to control criminal behavior, with the result being the disappearance of depression, paranoia, and related symptoms.

After completing a lecture on psychic abilities, I was cornered by a woman from the audience. She explained that she'd been trying for over a year to develop telepathic abilities, but that she had had difficulties with her concentration. She mentioned several physical problems which she felt might be hampering her efforts. I told her that these problems might indicate a low-blood-sugar condition. Several weeks later I received a letter from her thanking me profusely. The glucose test had confirmed hypoglycemia, and she was responding well to the dietary change. Six months later, a second letter informed me that she was receiving highly accurate information through telepathic awareness.

The body/mind connection: your mind will expand and grow as the result of a healthy body, and your body's peak performance comes through mind power.

A friend I'll call Peggy Stanner spent years participating in psychologists' therapy groups and exploring awareness techniques in a futile attempt to relieve her symptoms of insomnia, fatigue, and the feeling that things just weren't right. She was divorced during this time and received medication to relieve her anxiety and insomnia. On one occasion, her doctor hospitalized her for severe depression. Tests for low thyroid and other conditions revealed nothing. At her own insistence, she underwent a Glucose Tolerance Test. The results showed moderately severe hypoglycemia; after six weeks of the proper diet, the negative symptoms were gone.

A simple little condition that is easily solved, right? If you recognize it early enough and are willing to make permanent life-style changes, then that is correct.

However, if undiagnosed and untreated, hypoglycemia can indirectly kill you, as it is the forerunner of many of the worst degenerative diseases, such as diabetes and rheumatoid arthritis. If you do have a low-blood-sugar condition, one or more of the following symptoms will probably plague you with some regularity:

- Fatigue spells; drop in energy
- Weak feeling and desire for food
- Depression that lasts
- Cold sweats
- Night sweats
- Headaches
- Allergies
- Rapid beating of heart
- Mood swings and outbursts of temper
- Overall fear or feeling of insecurity
- Cold hands and feet
- Cramps in the legs
- Feeling old when you know you are not
- Just not feeling right; tired or weak
- Perspiring palms
- Disorientation
- Nausea
- Obesity
- Inner trembling
- Hungry right after a meal
- Blurred vision
- Mental confusion
- Incoherent speech
- Sudden phobias
- Fainting
- Convulsions
- Insomnia
- Waking in the night for no reason
- Falling asleep when you don't want to
- Sexual dysfunction
- Impotence or frigidity
- Irritability or crankiness
- Indigestion and gastrointestinal troubles
- Asthma

- Eczema
- Forgetfulness
- Suicidal tendencies

A logical question is: "Who *doesn't* have hypoglycemia?" However, since these are the most common general symptoms, they need to be mentioned. Having one of the symptoms doesn't necessarily mean you have low blood sugar, but it should cause you to think about it.

Another problem is mistaken diagnoses. There are numerous cases on record of patients who were mistakenly diagnosed as schizophrenic, neurotic, psychotic, alcoholic, or mentally disturbed, while in fact the patients were suffering from low blood sugar. Since many medical practitioners don't believe in the existence of hypoglycemia, they don't test for it; thus, the disease is often misdiagnosed. The following are a few more of the mistaken diagnoses that hypoglycemics have received:

- Cerebral arteriosclerosis
- Parkinson's syndrome
- Rheumatoid arthritis
- Chronic bronchial asthma
- Allergy
- Brain tumor
- Nervous breakdown
- Epilepsy
- Hives
- Neurosis
- Mental retardation
- Diabetes
- Senility
- Neurodermatitis
- Migraine

A thirty-five-year-old woman suffered from migraine headaches for years. Her husband was a career officer in the air force, so she was given every conceivable medical test at the finest military medical center in the country. After finding nothing physically abnormal, the medical practitioners suggested she see a psychiatrist. She followed their advice, and after a year of analysis, the headaches were more frequent and she was gaining weight. The stress and anxiety resulted in marital problems, and when her husband asked for a separation, she attempted suicide.

While the woman was hospitalized, a young nurse took an active interest in her case. The nurse was a vegetarian and nutrition-conscious, so she suggested a Glucose Tolerance Test. The results showed severe hypoglycemia.

Taking the nurse's suggestion, the woman followed a strict vegetarian diet for low blood sugar, instead of the standard high-protein diet. Two years have passed, and she reports: "I haven't had a migraine since I left the hospital. In fact, the only headache I've experienced was after sitting through a double-feature movie when I forgot my glasses."

The primary symptoms of fatigue, anxiety, depression, and mood changes can create excessive stress in a relationship, often breaking up a strained marriage.

If you want to find out for sure if you or someone you love has hypoglycemia, you must find a doctor who believes the disease exists and, ideally, one who has some background in dealing with it. The next step is a Six-Hour Glucose Tolerance Test (a three-hour test is insufficient) in conjunction with a complete medical examination.

THE SIX-HOUR GLUCOSE TOLERANCE TEST
To be given in A.M.

1. Patient fasts the night before.
2. A.M.: Blood test to determine the blood-sugar level.
3. Patient given a sugar solution to drink.
4. Once per hour for six hours, a blood test is taken to measure the blood-sugar level.
5. The rise and fall of the blood-sugar level will test the presence of hypoglycemia.

I suggest you purchase a book that will instruct you on how to read your own test. These books are available in health-food stores. If you don't find the right doctor, you're gambling with your relationships and your life, when some basic information will put you back in control.

Many people become aware of their condition before it contributes to a divorce. Diane Copen was not so fortunate. She was mistakenly diagnosed as neurotic. Her husband divorced her, and she lost a custody battle for two young sons before her case of severe hypoglycemia was correctly diagnosed and alleviated. By the time she was cured, there was nothing that could be done about the situation.

My own work with troubled couples suggests that half of the time, sexual encounters are conducted by exhausted people. They have forgotten their old enjoyment of sex, and they accept their current attitudes as a normal process of aging. Naturally, when hypoglycemia is present in only one partner, a problem is going to develop.

As part of a magazine assignment, I interviewed a twenty-eight-year-old woman who had lost interest in sex. The man she was living with felt personally rejected and began to pressure her for more sexual attention, which only made the situation worse. They eventually parted, and she spent months avoiding dates so she wouldn't have to face any sexual encounters. After more symptoms surfaced, she sought medical help and found that she had hypoglycemia. Today, after her cure, she reports that her sex drive is more intense than ever.

The most common form of hypoglycemia is usually caused by an improper diet of refined carbohydrates, and symptomatic reactions will often result from eating these foods. Additionally, the condition can be triggered by stress, and coffee, nicotine, or alcohol will aggravate it. Alcohol-induced hypoglycemia is also a prevalent situation today.

The traditional treatment of all but the most severe cases is the same: a special diet, vitamin supplements, and frequent small meals (five or six daily). Patients are asked to avoid all sugar and refined flour products and limit or eliminate altogether their intake of alcohol. At first, these restrictions may not sound difficult, but with a little investigation you will find that very few packaged foods are acceptable.

The average consumption of sugar in the United States is now 125 pounds per person per year—a teaspoon every thirty-five minutes around the clock. If you think that you don't eat much sugar, be aware that it is well disguised by the food manufacturers. There are virtually no meat sticks or sausages that do not contain sugar. Almost every cracker contains it, and many breakfast cereals are 50% or more sugar. It is in 95% of all canned goods—fruits, vegetables, soups, and other canned or packaged foods. Breads, salad dressings, Worcestershire sauce, hot dogs, and even most diet foods contain sugar. Be aware that food companies must list the ingriedients that make up their products in descending order of amount used, and they have become quite sneaky in hiding the actual amount of sugar by using table sugar as well as various other sugars, such as honey, sucrose, dextrose, corn syrup, lactose, etc. Thus, they spread the ingredients over the entire list. Otherwise, sugar would often have to be listed as the primary ingredient.

A simplified list of prohibited foods would include white sugar and everything made with it; ice cream, pastries, cookies, candies, and commercially baked breads; white flour and everything made with it, as well as unbleached flour—only whole grain products are acceptable; coffee and any product containing caffeine, which includes some pain relievers and even diet cola drinks; and alcohol and tobacco. In general, all processed, canned, refined, and other man-made foods should be avoided.

In *Hypoglycemia: A Better Approach,* Dr. Paavo Airola, a Swiss nutritionist and naturopathic physician, advocates a low-protein, high–"natural" carbohydrate diet. I have interviewed many ex-hypoglycemics who have successfully used Airola's diet to cure their illness.

The diet is also recommended by many nutritionists for general use. (See Diet and Nutrition section, Chapter 19.)

If you happen to be among the 50% who have a low-blood-sugar condition, Airola's diet may prove to be beneficial for you. It may force you to become physically fit.

Chapter 6

BODY TYPES

Dr. William Sheldon, author of *Varieties of Human Physique,* explains that function follows structure; in other words, there is a relationship between body build and personality. You act in accordance with your particular body type, and to act any other way would be foreign to your nature.

According to Sheldon and experts on nonverbal communication, mankind is divided into three groups called somatotypes, which have nothing to do with race, creed, or color. There is an athletic group, the muscular *mesomorphs,* who are the doers. The stouter group of *endomorphs* are the talkers, and the thin, small-boned race of *ectomorphs* are the thinkers. These basic categories are then divided into many additional subcategories that indicate the particular pathway that each person is likely to travel under average nutritional and pathological conditions.

It is generally agreed that your somatotype is the result of genetics, but there is also ample evidence to support the concept that the alteration of your physical structure will result in a corresponding personality change. In other words, the jovial overweight individual (endomorph) who successfully diets down to a standard body build (mesomorph) may become less of a talker and more a doer.

The easiest way to understand this theory is to see how well it fits you and those close to you. My first exposure to these concepts was in a nonverbal communication workshop conducted by Bruce Vaughan. As he discussed my somatotype (a combination of ectomorph 2 and 3), I realized Vaughan was describing in detail my basic personality. Later, when I heard Dr. George Sheehan relate this body type to running and to the general personality of runners, I decided to investigate further.

Of what value is this knowledge? Maybe if you're fighting your real self it will help you to relax and accept it. If you are an endomorph and are frustrated by your own chatter and procrastination, you will become aware of your genetic predisposition to this type of personality. If your husband is an ectomorph, and you'd like to see him become the gregarious life of the party, you'll realize that he is going to remain his same reflective self. An understanding of somatotypes helps you to be aware of your strengths and weaknesses, likes and dislikes, and manner of relating to people and situations. Knowledge of somatotypes can point the way to an appropriate life-style and even provide you with some solid clues as to the types of work and leisure that are most natural for you. It can even give you an idea of the sort of person you should marry.

Each somatotype has its special qualities, and harmony among the types is often difficult to achieve. Each reacts in ways that other types find annoying, distressing, or even dangerous. Although somatotypes are seen, rather than unseen, influences, I include them because few people are aware of their powerful innate effect.

In one of his initial statistical research projects involving hundreds of people, Dr. Sheldon found 9% of his study population ectomorphs (thin), 12% mesomorphs (athletic), and 7% endomorphs (heavy). The remaining 72% were mixtures of the three basic types.

In his book *The Atlas of Men,* Dr. Sheldon provides detailed information on forty-three somatotypes, with many variations. Other researchers have categorized them in different ways. For the sake of simplification, I will break this understanding down into seven very generalized categories:

1. Ectomorph (Very thin)
2. Ectomorph (Thin)
3. Ectomorph (Slender)
4. Mesomorph (Normal athletic)
5. Mesomorph (Stocky athletic)
6. Endomorph (Stout)
7. Endomorph (Heavy)

1. Ectomorph (Very thin):

Very thin ectos are quiet, sensitive, and introverted. They mind their own business, and you will rarely see them in the center of activities. They tend to be pale and are rarely successful in muscle-oriented endeavors. They are thinkers and usually do well at academic and artistic pursuits, often achieving scholastic brilliance. Many become scientists or engineers, or take up related "exacting" careers. Ectos dislike small talk and react to stress by withdrawing. They prefer sports without physical contact, such as running, tennis, or bowling, and seem to be able to eat anything without ever growing fat. The ecto often matures late and tends to fade rapidly. This type tends to break down mentally more easily than the others. Schizophrenia is the predominant affliction.

2. Ectomorph (Thin):

The thin ecto is agile, resourceful, and often tends to lead a defiant, unconventional way of life. Although too brittle for direct fighting, thin ectomorphs are usually muscular enough to feel at ease in a bathing suit. As loners, they prefer an extremely private life-style and will always attempt to avoid crowds unless they are leading the activities. Thin ectos often display an intense drive; they are perfectionists and tend to be materially oriented. They are detached individuals and prefer to-the-point communication without small talk. You will usually find them in aesthetic or technical career situations. Although sometimes competent in athletic areas, this type will tend toward sports like cross-country running or tennis. They are likely to be long-lived.

3. Ectomorph (Slender):

Slender ectos are well coordinated and more powerful than the previous category. They are efficient fighters and do well in athletic competition that does not require resilient bounce or heavy punishment. Although reserved, people of this body type are assertive, competitive, optimistic, and more open to involvement with others, needing recognition from their peers. Slender ectos want security and are sticklers in careers requiring detailed work. Although hard workers, they like to escape and play.

4. Mesomorph (Normal athletic):

Mesomorphs are doers, usually exhibiting self-sufficient, competitive, and aggressive character traits. Their athletic bodies are designed for muscular activity, and they welcome a strenuous way of life. Their personalities are open, cheerful, and energetic. A meso must succeed at his vocation, or life will become uncomfortable for everyone around him. As pragmatic, materially oriented people, mesos excel in standard business and will do whatever is necessary to get the job done. Many professional athletes are mesos, and you can depend on the fact that mesos will react to stress by taking action. Although they exhibit a hard leanness in youth, people of this somatotype tend to soften up appreciably with advancing age. Mesos tend to be exhibitionists and love to play outdoors.

5. Mesomorph (Stocky athletic):

The stocky mesomorph is likened in body type to both cats and bears, having the agility of a cat and the strength of a bear. These are the powerful athletes who were often slim when younger and will become quite fat in older age. They are usually considered delightful companions and relish social activities. Thus, they make ideal salespeople and are usually quite successful as a result of their aggressiveness. Stocky mesos need recognition more than they require material benefits. If a stocky mesomorph does not have a heavy-duty cardiovascular system, he will be a statistical candidate for coronary trouble and related problems.

6. Endomorph (Stout):

Stout endomorphs are the talkers of the world and are compared in body type to grizzly bears or seals. They are champions at wrestling, and their general physical pattern is that of the mountain-dwelling people of the Alps. Stout endos are gregarious, happy people with a zest for life. You will find large numbers of this body type at the beach, where they are buoyantly active and surpass all others at leaping in and out of the water. They are often procrastinators, being good at originating concepts but needing other people to finish for them. Their need to be recognized is a primary motivation. People of this type often bald and gain weight easily after college age. Few are long-lived unless physically active.

7. Endomorph (Heavy):

Heavy endomorphs are sentimental optimists who love to talk even more than they love to eat. They are built for service, not speed, and after college age they typically gain weight on a steep curve until their early forties. At one end of this category are the football players who play the sturdy team positions; at the other end, body types are soft and round. Heavy endos are people-oriented and have a primary need to be recognized and accepted. They love parties and visitors. They will procrastinate in most situations, but they are extremely generous and will volunteer to help anyone. The heavy endos are not long-lived unless heroic dietary and exercise measures are taken.

Chapter 7

BRAIN-WAVE SIMILARITIES
AND PSYCHIC INPUT

Owing to our involvement with the metaphysical world, Trenna and I are often asked to recommend a good psychic. The usual reason is the person's belief that the psychic can solve his problem. In such situations, I usually suggest that the individual use his own power to solve his own problem. When this is not possible, he should seek out an exceptionally responsible psychic. Usually, the term *psychic* is a catchall for telepath, medium, trance medium, channel, spiritualist, gypsy, or card reader. An explanation of how psychics work is an introduction to one of the lesser recognized unseen influences.

As an introductory aid for individually directed hypnosis sessions, I often use a brain-wave synchronizer. This is a medical instrument with a strobing light that can be varied to synchronize with beta, alpha, theta, and delta brain-wave levels, which are measured in cycles per second of brain activity. The subject sits in a recliner in front of the synchronizer while I vary the light pulsation. Through the subject's color perception, I can lock in on his brain wave, and the device, accompanied by verbal induction techniques, helps to lull him into a deep hypnotic sleep.

Dr. J. Dudley Chapman reported on his research work with the brain-wave synchronizer in a major medical journal. When the doctor and his team worked with subjects in a darkened room, 55% to 69% of the time the medical team knew the subjects' thoughts, ideas, and words before they were verbalized. There was an extremely high degree of ESP, and the deeper the subjects' hypnotic trance, the more accurate the telepathic connection became. It also became clear that the more highly charged emotions were more readily "felt" by the hypnotist; for example, any problems that were sexual, marital, or socially unacceptable in nature.

The technical explanation for this phenomenon is brain-wave synchrony. The subject watches the flashing light that is synchronized to his brain wave, the most common wave being alpha-6. The hypnotist watches his subject, but in the dark room, the strobing light reflects off the subject's face, resulting in the hypnotist entering an altered state of consciousness as well. If the hypnotist's brain wave is anywhere near that of the subject, the pulsation will cause his wave to alter and fall into sync with the subject's. If the two brain waves are synchronized, ESP is highly probable.

A psychic has the ability, consciously or unconsciously, to alter his own brain wave to match yours and then to read your mind. Often, someone will go to a psychic, and the reading will be amazingly accurate. The subject is so impressed that he eagerly tells his friend to go to the psychic for a reading, that he's fantastically accurate. The friend makes an appointment, but he is disappointed with the results of the session. The psychic seems to miss on everything. Why? The psychic's brain wave was quite close to that of the first individual. We'll assume that the subject was alpha-6 and the psychic, alpha-8. It was easy to alter the two steps, to synchronize with the subject and thus open a telepathic channel. In the second situation, the friend was an alpha-3. This wave was too different for the psychic to synchronize with, and thus a clear channel was impossible. No psychic in the world is equally accurate for everyone he or she reads.

In my seminars, I have explored this same concept with sound, recording the cycles-per-second sound of mid-beta (approximately 850 beats per minute) and over a five-minute period slowing it down to the bottom of alpha (approximately 145 beats per minute). In some situations, I've combined this technique with a standard verbal hypnosis induction, while in others, I've simply asked the participants to "become the sound." In both cases, 95% of the group have gone into an altered state of consciousness.

Your mind attempts to synchronize with a visual or audio stimulus of the proper pulsation. Men and women who have been together for a length of time often develop considerable ESP between each other. They come to know accurately what the other is going to do or say. This could simply be due to the fact that they know each other quite well, but I don't think so. We know that extrasensory perception is a reality, and my own understanding and tests cause me to believe that superconscious communication also exists.

I believe that when two people spend years in close proximity, both of their brain waves alter to a common wave, and that individuals living and sleeping together year after year are superconsciously seeking synchronization. The closer the two brain waves were at the beginning of the relationship, the faster this synchronization will transpire.

Another way to look at this concept is to use the radio analogy. We function on a particular frequency, and it may be that we feel a natural intuitive attraction or bond with others on or close to our own "wavelength." Yet, we have the ability to switch stations or to work with other stations to achieve a mutually acceptable frequency.

On two occasions, I asked the following question in a seminar we were conducting: "Are there any couples attending who feel they have a strong extrasensory bond?" Of the eighteen couples I worked with, most had been married for over five years. In using the brain-wave synchronizer to establish their levels, I found that seven had identical brain-wave levels, eight were no more than two points apart, and the remaining three were within three points of each other. These results are so far beyond mathematical chance that they show high probability of a "frequency attraction" or evidence of altered waves due to close proximity. However, the only conclusive evidence will result from monitoring a test group of couples from the beginning of their relationships.

The more psychically sensitive an individual is, the more likely he or she is to be influenced by the thoughts and feelings of others. I contend that 20% of the population are extremely empathic without realizing it. These people believe that all their thoughts, feelings, and emotions, no matter how irrational, originate solely from within. For an example, a woman attends the symphony and is seated in the auditorium next to a man who is in bad health and worried sick about his runaway teenage son. Soon, the woman begins to feel a strong sense of anxiety which she cannot relate to any cause. She is picking it up from the man next to her. An empath is very likely to receive in this way without brain-wave similarities, but assuming these two subjects are both alpha-6, then an even more intensified telepathic channel would probably result.

Those involved in developing their psychic abilities are also honing their empathic skills and should be prepared for situations of this kind. Often in seminars, after working at explorations of altered states of consciousness for several days, I have observed natural sensitives blossom overnight and begin exhibiting undeniable extrasensory abilities. They are usually so thrilled and awed by their new awareness that they don't listen to my admonitions as to the full meaning of their situation.

Let me get back to the concept of superconscious communication and how that relates to psychic work and the unseen influences. Both Trenna and I can read tarot with a high degree of accuracy. We never do it professionally, but on occasion, we have worked with friends in an attempt to discover unknowns about a particular situation. Before we begin, we always tell the querent: "There is nothing magic or mystical about the cards; they are simply a methodology which easily

68

allows the knowledge that is already in your superconscious mind to filter down into your consciousness. Tea leaves would be equally effective if I'd develop a symbol system to interpret them. You could also drop pine needles on the floor, and if I had developed an interpretative system, they could tell us the same thing as the tarot cards. The important thing to remember is that the cards will tell you of potentials that exist—potentials you are giving power to and moving toward, but which are not absolutes. Any situation can be mitigated, altered, or negated. Everything I tell you, you will already be aware of intuitively, for the information is coming from you."

Upon reading his cards, I told a friend, "You're soon going to be getting a job offer for much more money, and if you accept it, you'll be moving out of state."

Two weeks later, he received the offer, and his reaction to me was, "I hadn't even thought about changing jobs, and this opportunity came from California, so how could I have known about it intuitively or superconsciously?"

"Very simply. The man who offered you the job was already thinking about offering it to you when I read the cards. The minute he thought of you, your superconscious mind was aware of it, and the information could be channeled through the reading. Another explanation would be that he had a need and so did you, although you weren't consciously aware of it. Thus, superconscious contact was made well in advance of conscious contact. Look at it as the want-ad section of a newspaper that is read by your higher mind. He advertised in it, and you saw the ad and decided to apply. At that point, negotiations became psychically apparent. Do realize, however, that at the time of the card reading, it was a potential, not an absolute."

The primary problem in taking your troubles to a psychic is that people tend to believe everything a psychic says, and no one in this field is 100% accurate. An even more important consideration is that most people dwell on the negative side of things. The psychic says, "I hate to tell you this, but you're going to be getting a divorce," or, "I'm afraid you're in for a bad auto accident, so be careful driving. It's all right though, you're going to survive." Now, nobody is capable of forgetting predictions like that. Maybe the psychic did pick up on a potential, but by making the prediction, he almost assures the negative outcome, as the poor subject will dwell on the forthcoming event. The subject will give it so much power that he is sure to create the effect.

I have spent considerable time with some of the finest psychics in this country, but for the reasons just mentioned, I usually tell them that I want to talk and not hear any predictions. I would say these "major names" have predicted as absolute fact about thirty important situations in my life and were absolutely wrong. The actual outcomes have often been direct reversals of the predictions. Of course, many of their prophecies were accurate, but after years of involvement, I know to take what they say as nothing more than an "interesting potential." I listen to my own heart and my own higher self, and find I'm in much better hands.

There are, however, numerous ways that a psychic's input can be of considerable value. Often, they have helped me to unravel complicated cases and investigate situations from other perspectives. The point to remember is that this information should be considered a possibility worthy of investigation, but never an absolute.

Some friends of ours, two couples, stopped by our house on a Sunday afternoon. They asked Trenna and me to read for them, explaining only that they were involved in a business deal with someone else and that they wondered how it would go. We used the tarot as the methodology and did four card spreads. It was immediately obvious to Trenna and me that there was a heavy affair going on between one of the men and the wife of his business partner and friend. Naturally, we didn't discuss this in the presence of all four of our visitors. We did talk about other less explosive findings and about the fact that the business situation was not what it appeared to be on the surface. We actually described the man they were dealing with and advised further investigation.

Within a week, we were told that the business deal fell apart, causing our friends to lose a good deal of money. The man we described in our tarot reading was the deceiver. In addition, within the month, the love affair became known, resulting in two vicious divorces and the end of the business partnership. In this case, we were right about what was verbalized and what wasn't, but we could have been wrong. It would be easy to be irresponsible to the querent by telling him something that would preoccupy him, thus causing his fears to come true. Therefore, I seldom suggest that someone go to a psychic. If an individual is depressed, I almost always advise him or her not to go, for it is even more likely that the psychic will pick up depressed impressions. Thus, by forecasting negative situations, they will perpetrate more negativity.

Of course, there are always psychics who are simply fooling you. Most psychics will pull some accurate information from your superconscious, often just enough to get you to believe they are "magic." Then you'll believe all the unverifiable data you're fed. I'll wager that half the people who have ever had a psychic reading have been told that they have problems they are later unable to verify. However, the subject will openly endorse the psychic's wisdom by telling all his friends how he was saved from his problems. Following a typical pattern of psychic involvement, people inform the world of everything that the psychic was accurate about or that they think he was accurate about, but they never tell anyone about his misses. I guess it is simply human nature to want to dramatize one's stories and experiences, but this is hardly an objective position. The obvious result is greater advertising for the psychic, who is fully aware of this human quirk.

To summarize, I would say that if you know you can be objective, and you have a valid reason for a reading, then find a good, responsible psychic and use the information he provides as an investigative tool or as an indication of a potential you can mitigate. If you are happy and content in your life, stay away from readings. You might be told something that will make you unhappy, and it might not even be valid. If you're unhappy, then stay away for the reason I've already described. Remember, too, that *you* are psychic. Everyone has these abilities, and you can usually trust your own intuition much more than another's predictions.

Chapter 8

BODY RHYTHMS

We are all subjected to rules prescribed by our own nature. We must be aware of these rules if we expect to be able to recover properly from illness and lead healthy lives. These are internal body rhythms, which are seemingly regulated by our life-style, and the unseen external rhythms of gravity, electromagnetic fields, light waves, air pressure, and sound. The cycles of night and day, the moon and the flow of the tide, the seasonal changes, and many other factors are all rhythms that affect us.

The human body is constantly experiencing hundreds and maybe thousands of cyclical effects. Even the simple act of breathing works alternately in a cycle. Normally, you will breathe through one nostril for about three hours while the tissues of the other are slightly engorged. An exchange occurs in three hours, and you will breathe predominantly through the other nostril. If you doubt this, just breathe in slowly, and you will notice that one nostril is more open than the other.

Circadian rhythms are the important organizing principles of our physiology. Your body temperature, blood pressure, respiration, pulse, blood sugar, hemoglobin levels, and amino acid levels rise and fall in cycles over a twenty-four-hour period. One result of this activity shows up in psychomotor coordination.

Extensive tests have proven that there are different times of the day during which you perform better mentally and physically, although your effort would seem equal in your eyes. The time required for a specific task would vary according to the type of challenge, and often test situations would show as much as 100% variation in areas of mental concentration. Physical exertion and sports performance are also radically affected. By keeping notes or a diary of activities and performances, an individual can begin to chart his own rhythms and thus become more productive and effective.

Physiological differences are likely to be found in the circadian rhythms of "morning" and "night" people—those individuals who arise easily and function best in the early hours and those who come to life and show optimum performance in the evening. Yet, I believe that these rhythms can be altered by positive changes in life-style. Through most of our adult lives, Trenna and I have been night people. We always hated to get up in the morning and struggled through the early hours in a sort of daze. Afternoons improved our energies, and by evening, our creative juices were flowing. Bedtime was usually around two or three in the morning. Then a few years ago, we began to make many life-style changes. We shifted from the standard American diet by first eliminating all sugar, coffee, and other undesirable food items and then by gradually adopting a healthful vegetarian diet. At the same time, we changed from a sedentary life-style to one in which we were actively involved in karate and daily running. These changes took place over a two-year period.

Today, we arise easily early in the morning and are immediately ready to tackle creative tasks. By evening, we know our performance is less than the best, and we're ready for bed between ten and midnight. I've talked with many others who have experienced similar effects after life-style changes.

Circadian rhythms also affect the way your system reacts to drugs. Just as people are not equally resistant

74

to all kinds of stress at all hours, they also do not react to drugs the same way at different times of the day. A drug with marginal reactions at one hour can be as much as 70% more toxic at another hour. Drugs are not tested for accordance with circadian rhythms, and if the doctor or patient is not aware of body rhythms in administering strong drugs, serious consequences can result.

Each year, thousands of people die of an overdose of narcotics or other drugs. Suicide perhaps, but not by intention, for the wide variance in toxicity can often kill if the drug is taken at the rhythm point of least resistance. The assumption that a patient needs the same amount of antihistamine, barbiturate, or antibiotic at all hours of the day is simply not in keeping with contemporary research.

Rhythms of the nervous system may explain why sick people need stronger dosages of pain-killers at certain hours of the night and early morning. There is probably a rhythmic change in the tolerance of pain. We are only beginning to understand this complicated aspect of human physiology.

Ultradian rhythms are shorter than the circadian cycles and occur with a higher frequency. Infradian rhythms are longer cycles of a week, a month, or more. There are also annual rhythms that affect everyone differently, and patterns of general influence are revealed in statistics compiled by the Minnesota Department of Health. As an example, these statistics show that deaths from arteriosclerosis peak in January, while suicides and suicide attempts peak around May. Seasonal trends are also found among the types of depression that might be related to hormone regulation. For example, those with endogenous depression or manic-depressive illnesses tend to be sicker in autumn and spring.

Another interesting concept is the way that body metabolism relates to time. It certainly qualifies as an unseen influence. Dr. Hudson Hoagland is the foremost researcher in the exploration of this subject. In his book *The Voices of Time,* he relates that he became interested in this field when his wife had a 140° fever and asked him to go to the drugstore. He was gone only twenty minutes, but she insisted that he had taken hours. Intrigued, he began to test her time perception, knowing that as a trained musician she normally had a fine sense of time. After twenty-five tests, he found that when she had a fever, time slowed down, but that when her temperature was normal, her sense of timing was accurate.

Extensive testing followed, with results suggesting that time may be modulated by a metabolic-chemical pacemaker system in the brain. An interesting aspect of this knowledge is that there is a decline in the rate at which you consume oxygen and a slowing of metabolism as you progress from childhood to maturity. Thus, time may seem to pass very slowly for a child but very quickly for an adult.

A man who spent two months in an underground cavern conducting a research project reported such severe memory loss that it was often hard for him to recall what he had done a few minutes before. On emerging from the cavern, he was given a physical examination, which showed that his metabolism was greatly slowed down and that his condition of torpor was one of semihibernation. He explained that time seemed to have passed very quickly, without his being aware of it, in the silence and darkness. He claimed that for the most part, he didn't dwell on the past or the future but only seemed to exist within the present—the hostile darkness.

If time speeds up when metabolism slows down and slows down when metabolism speeds up, time could be a variable experience for cold-blooded animals. The physiochemical result would be that warm summer days would seem very long and the winter's hibernation a night's sleep.

The metabolic rate of very heavy people is often slowed down, so it may follow that they experience the passage of time more rapidly than their friends of a normal build. The reverse would be true with those who have a high metabolic rate.

Phase shifting is a condition that affects most people on an occasional basis, but millions are affected regularly, and the potential consequences have never been well publicized. Researchers investigating body time believe that disruptions caused by certain kinds of schedules and travel can result in such serious consequences as mental and physical illness. When our biological clock is suddenly desynchronized with the world around us, it can take days for our cardiac rhythms to readjust, and our adrenal hormones may take as long as two weeks to reset to a new schedule of sleep and rest.

A pilot flying an irregular schedule of nights and days or flying an east/west schedule is a good example of this problem. Extensive tests have shown premature aging in such pilots, and other degenerative conditions appear more regularly in east/west pilots who are always out of sync with their environment due to time changes.

To a lesser degree, we experience this problem as jet lag from occasional airline flights. Individuals finding themselves in this situation drag themselves around with a body whose heart rate and urine composition indicate a state more like sleep than waking. The blood corticosterone and urine electrolytes are out of phase with internal rhythms, which explains why the government and businesses have their personnel rest for twenty-four hours after a long jet trip before conducting any important transactions.

Some overseas pilots maintain their stability by remaining on their home time, sleeping and waking only according to their normal schedule, regardless of the time in the foreign country. Individuals can cope with eastward travel by going to bed progressively earlier before the trip to minimize the loss of time. The opposite would be the case before a long westerly trip.

Any change in your normal routine and schedule which results in desynchronization is highly undesirable from a mental and physical health perspective. People who live a life of chaotic schedules, long days, and excessive jet travel are hurting themselves far more than they probably realize. If they override with drugs the inevitable signs of fatigue and desynchronization, they are rapidly moving toward long-term illness.

Another important phase shift consideration is the job with an alternating schedule, such as a factory situation in which you work three days, then two nights. Any form of schedule shifting is one of the worst things an individual can do to his body. The practice desynchronizes the natural body rhythms, and there is an unusually high incidence of ulcers and hypertension among those whose jobs require phase shifting. Extremely high divorce rates are also seen among this group, and in several research studies, the practice has been proven to cause failing health in middle-aged individuals. Some people can adjust better than others. One test of 1000 workers showed that 55% were capable of the necessary internal adjustment.

We must moderate the shifting and the changes in our lives if we seek optimum health. Any situation causing stress or any situation of change forces an individual to adjust. The frequency and degree of these changes have been shown to affect our well-being. This discovery has been well documented by Drs. Thomas H. Holmes and Richard Rahe, who developed the stress point scale. The death of a spouse is at the top of the scale, with a value of 100 points. Marriage is rated at 50 points, the birth of a child 39 points, and lesser situations, such as vacations or the purchase of a new home, are each assigned point values in keeping with the doctors' research.

Through their work with thousands of Americans and Japanese, it became obvious to the doctors that individuals with a high number of points in one year's time were more likely to develop some serious illness in the following year. The higher the score, the more severe the illness was likely to be.

Thus, the pace of life and rate of change seem to predict illness. We pay quite a toll for our chaotic lives, for crowding, pollution, and noise. The results are often psychosomatic, or emotionally induced, illness. Public Health Survey No. 1000, Series 11 #37, studied

6,672 people and revealed that one out of five had either had a nervous breakdown or felt the potential of a breakdown.

The ecosystem of human life is deteriorating, and eventually medicine will have to become holistic in its scope, utilizing knowledge of body rhythms and synchronization to be more effective at healing. Someday, we hope to have accurate preventive guidance. Job scheduling will be more humane, and job screening will be able to match the proper person to the proper position. Drug testing must consider circadian rhythmicity, and a reevaluation of medical diagnoses should be conducted.

We as individuals must also accept more responsibility for our own well-being instead of relying upon doctors to save us. We can attempt to ascertain the reasons for our illnesses by assessing our own habits and lifestyle. By keeping notes recording their uneven dispositions, their undulating moods, changes, stresses, and numerous related effects, many people have become aware of patterns. Adverse symptoms can be generated in many people within a few minutes by desynchronization of one of the circadian rhythms.

Biorhythms

Many readers may expect me to include biorhythms as an unseen influence, but after extensive investigation of this concept, I have concluded that biorhythms are more mythical than real. "But they work. Just let me tell you a couple of my experiences" is the advocate's usual response. I have personally had the same sort of experiences, which I will attempt to explain.

In 1887, Wilhelm Fliess published his formula for the use of biological rhythms. His premise was that we are all bisexual, and he related our biological cycles to male and female rhythms that he claimed affected both genders equally. Fliess linked the twenty-three- and twenty-eight-day cycles to changes occurring in the mucosal lining of the nose. He related nasal irritation to neurotic symptoms and sexual abnormalities. This attracted Sigmund Freud, and had it not been for Freud's interest, Fliess's concepts would probably have faded into a fitting obscurity.

Fliess developed a medical practice in which he diagnosed ills by inspecting the patient's nose and applying cocaine to what he called the "genital cells" in the nasal interior. Add this type of wisdom to the man's unsophisticated understanding of simple mathematics, and you have the scientific foundation for biorhythms.

The mass interest in the biorhythm concept has stimulated research of the subject at prestigious scientific centers. A spokesman for one laboratory claims the public is being duped. He explained that there is no scientific basis for these cycles. In fact, the cycles are inconsistent with those biological rhythms that have been substantiated scientifically.

Often, advocates claim ridiculous evidence to support their belief and accept only those cases which tend to prove the validity of biorhythms, while dismissing all other views. As an example, they maintain that John F. Kennedy's intellectual rhythm was at a critical point on the day of the assassination and believe this may have influenced his decision to ride in the motorcade. With all three cycles crossing the zero-flux line, you will end up with at least five critical days per month, and at least 80% of the time you'll have one of your cycles in a negative position below the line. With statistics like that, you can blame almost everything that happens to you on biorhythms.

The biorhythm books cite great statistical studies supportive of this concept. Yet, the documentation and controls for most of these studies are nonexistent, so it is impossible for researchers to check their validity. From a statistical perspective, the figures are hopelessly inconsistent and usually represent small numbers of cases.

In 1975, an air force study of 8,625 pilots involved in aircraft accidents, both military and civilian, found no correlation between the accident dates and the pilots' critical days. In 1973, the Workman's Compensation Board of British Columbia conducted the largest biorhythm accident study of all by examining 13,285 on-the-job accidents. Only 20% of these accidents happened on critical days, which is the statistical percentage of chance.

There are many mistakes in the examples of major case histories in some of the best-selling biorhythm books. The authors often stretch a point to make a point, and in some cases stretch a couple of days to make the picture more dramatic. Most amusing is the fact that some of these inaccuracies have been copied by author after author, all of whom have relied solely upon the word of the original book.

The books also talk about companies that have instituted safety programs that take biorhythms into account. What the books fail to explain is that most companies dropped their programs after a short trial because statistically, they made no difference. One spokesman for a trucking insurance company that does use biorhythms explains: "Anything that may make a driver more safety conscious is worth a try. If it works and safety consciousness is improved, it doesn't matter whether biorhythm cycles are correct or not."

Chronobiologists do agree that we have physical, emotional, and intellectual rhythms but feel that these are not as simple as biorhythms and are not related to our birthdays. It is agreed that the rhythms are variable and would be different for different people. To explore the concept, you must chart your own emotions, moods, clumsiness, et cetera. Within a few months, you may have a better understanding of yourself.

How can biorhythms be disclaimed when they seem to work? Two ways. First, as an example, I once charted biorhythms for a friend and his wife. He was a few days late in picking them up from me, and during that time, his wife had an automobile accident. When we checked the day against the chart, it was a critical day. Explanation: mathematical chance.

The second argument is the unlimited power of the mind. Your mind is superconsciously capable of things

81

you cannot imagine and is also highly suggestible. Once exposed to the biorhythm premise, it could calculate your chart out for the rest of your life in a matter of seconds. I guarantee to you that the knowledge is retained forever. You couldn't even imagine accomplishing such a thing consciously, but be aware that brain researchers claim your brain has 200,000 times the capacity of the largest computer ever built. If you consciously feed your higher mind belief in the biorhythm concept, it will accept it and act upon it. Being a good computer, it will act according to the programming it is fed. Thus, if you have a double-critical day on August 28, 1985, your superconscious already knows it and will cooperate by creating the programmed negative effect.

The best thing you can do to deprogram unnecessary future effects is to send strong messages of disbelief in biorhythms to your higher mind.

Chapter 9

POSITIVE AND NEGATIVE IONS

"I don't know what is wrong with me. I've been looking forward to attending this seminar for months, yet since I arrived in Arizona two days ago, I've felt some sort of anxiety I don't understand. In fact, I just feel kind of physically 'blah' all over," she explained.

The first seminar session wasn't due to start for a few hours. Participants were registering, and several, wearing name badges, were sitting around the swimming pool area of the Scottsdale resort hotel. The sad look on the face of this attractive middle-aged woman caught my attention, so I stopped to introduce myself and ask how she was doing. At first, she said that she felt fine, but when I persisted, she responded truthfully.

"Maybe you're just feeling anxious about the regression sessions and explorations we're going to be doing," I offered.

"Oh, no, I've been regressed several times. I know it isn't that," she said. "Maybe it's a flu bug, but it certainly has terrible timing. This is supposed to be a vacation."

Her name badge indicated that she was from Cleveland, Ohio. "This is just a hunch," I said, "but before the seminar begins, why don't you either take a very long shower or go swimming and remain close to the waterfall at the end of the pool." She looked at me very strangely. "These hot desert winds we've been having for the last couple of weeks charge the air with electricity in a way that creates adverse physical effects in some people. Spraying water cancels out the effect."

Later that day, she explained that she felt fine, even exhilarated, while around the water, but within a short time after leaving that environment, the previous feelings returned. Obviously this woman, accustomed to a Cleveland environment, was being adversely affected by the abundance of positive ions in the air. Since that experience, when the winds are blowing and out-of-staters are involved, I always explain this situation to participants during the first session of any Arizona or California seminar. In several medical and scientific journals, Dr. Felix Sulman reported the results of research work with several hundred human subjects. Air ions had a *significant* biological effect on approximately 25% of the population, and a *considerable* effect on the next 50%; the remaining 25% were not affected when the ion balance was upset.

In his book *The Ion Effect,* Fred Soyka explains how his research began as an attempt to prove to himself that he was neither a manic-depressive nor a hypochondriac. For ten years after moving to Geneva, Switzerland, he suffered extreme anxiety, depression, and physical illness. Neither doctors nor psychiatrists could explain these effects, which became progressively worse until Soyka discovered that the foehn winds were responsible. When he returned to New York, all his symptoms disappeared.

Positive ions caused by hot, dry winds create the negative effects already described. In addition, they are also associated with numerous maladies, such as loss of good sense, hot flashes, internal tremors, vertigo, sleeplessness, irritability, migraine, nausea, palpitations, and swelling. The eventual debilitating effects could indirectly result in death.

An excess of negative ions in the air results in reverse effects for many people: mental alertness, increased productivity, a feeling of well-being, increased sexual drive. The air is always highly charged with negative ions immediately following a rain, and we've all experienced the exhilaration in taking a deep breath outside after a storm.

So, what are ions? They're minute, invisible, electrically charged air particles. Normal air is balanced at a ratio of 5 positive to 4 negative ions. Along a beach where waves are breaking forcefully enough to throw water into the air, negative ions are twice as prevalent as positive ions. It is this ratio that the majority of the population will find highly desirable. They will feel better mentally and physically and will react with noticeably higher spirits. No wonder Niagara Falls, which offers 100 times the normal negative ion count in the air, is such a popular honeymoon location.

When the dry "witches' winds" blow, the air can be charged with up to 33 positive ions to every negative ion, which explains how these winds came to be known worldwide as "the winds which blow no good." In the California deserts, they are called the "Santa Ana"; in the Rocky Mountain regions, the "chinook"; in Italy, the "sirocco." They exist in different areas all over the world. Accident rates are said to double in France when the dry winds blow, and in Switzerland, the authorities accept the blowing of foehn winds during the commission of a crime as mitigating evidence in a court of law.

Some researchers are concerned that the heaviest doses of positive ions are found in polluted city environments, which act as collectors for negative ions. Noxious fumes, automobile exhausts, cigarette smoke, dust, and soot attract and neutralize neg-ions or reverse their charge. Steel and concrete buildings also absorb them. Synthetic materials, such as those used in modern buildings, furniture, and clothing, attract and trap these desirable ions, while the positive static charge of plastics reduces them further. The result is that large population centers are becoming more charged with positive ions.

We need 1,000 neg-ions per cubic centimeter to function at our optimum. Recent tests have shown ion counts to be below 100 per cubic centimeter inside some office buildings and in certain homes within populous areas. Medical findings alone would tell us that this is a highly undesirable situation. Negative ions are believed to kill germs. Using both charged and uncharged rooms in burn center research, it was found that neg-ions lessened infection, dried the burns faster, and accelerated healing with fewer scars. Other medical reports indicate patients felt less pain in neg-ion charged rooms. Bronchial asthma, allergies, sinus problems, hay fever, and migraine problems have also been relieved with this therapy. Neg-ions seem to act upon our capacity to absorb and utilize oxygen. They are known to promote alpha brain waves.

Some work environments use negative-ion generators. This results in fatigue reduction which, when combined with increased attentiveness, makes for higher productivity. In Germany and Russia, such generators are common in government buildings, hospitals, schools, factories, and public businesses such as restaurants. Individuals use them in their homes and automobiles. As a friend of mine who toured Russia told me, "The Russians consider a neg-ion generator more important than a refrigerator."

Although we seem to be less ion-conscious than much of the world, the U.S. Government has equipped our nuclear submarines with ion generators. Back in World War II, Luftwaffe planes were neg-ionized in an attempt to reduce pilot fatigue.

Bishop James Pike is well known to most metaphysically oriented people as the controversial Episcopalian Bishop of San Francisco who resigned in 1968, a few months before he was to be expelled for heresy due to his outspoken beliefs. Pike's involvement with medium Arthur Ford created international news.

In 1969, at the age of fifty-six, Pike and his wife Dianne embarked on a trip into a roadless Israeli desert in an ordinary passenger car without a guide or provisions. The car got stuck; they attempted to walk back out of the desert, but Pike became too tired. Dianne went on alone in an attempt to find help. She walked for ten hours and was rescued, but it took a massive land and air search that lasted for five days to find James Pike's body. He had died of hunger, thirst, and exhaustion.

An Israeli doctor who examined the case concluded that the prevailing *sharav* (dry winds) may have influenced the decision to go into the desert. It is believed that positive ions break down serotonin in the bloodstream. Pike's system could have been thrown out of balance by even a modest overdose of serotonin.

Following my lecture on unseen influences at a New Age Festival in Los Angeles, a couple in their early thirties came up to tell me of their experiences with the ion effect. The man explained that he had worked for a mortgage company in the Midwest. The offices were located in a remodeled wooden building on the edge of the central downtown sector. The company was expanding, and the decision was made to move into a new steel and glass high-rise bank building that had just been completed in the center of the city. No sooner had the company moved in than the employee climate changed—bickering was common and everyone seemed to overreact. The air seemed so stale in the afternoon that often this man felt light-headed and out of sorts. A friend suggested to him that it could be a situation of ion depletion and might be alleviated with a small negative-ion generator set on his desk.

"From the moment I began using the negative-ion generator, I felt fine," he explained. "It was as different as black and white. Then the word got around, and my office became the most popular place in the company, especially in the late afternoons when the depletion was at its worst. Everybody could tell the difference. The owners decided to ionize the entire office. No sooner had they installed the equipment than the old harmony returned to the company. That was just a little over a year ago, before I accepted a job offer here in Los Angeles."

Further investigation reveals the following facts about ions. In new buildings that are sealed, fresh air can only be channeled through the central heating/air-conditioning ducts, and as air travels through the bending metal channels, a friction is created that extracts most of the ions from the air. When the air finally arrives through the vent, only a small percentage of positive ions remains. Any last negative ions are quickly absorbed by the synthetic carpeting and materials in the office. The result is a continual "witch's wind," and it certainly blows no good for the employees trapped within the environment. Naturally, some buildings are far worse than others. This often has to do with the distance the air has to travel. The fortieth floor would most likely be more depleted than the first floor.

On another occasion after a seminar where I lectured on unseen influences, one of the participants went home to New York to investigate the ion effect in her own life. She found that she had a problem with ion depletion, but not because she worked in a hermetically sealed building. It was a result of the East Coast summer humidity. She suffered from a respiratory allergy, but since electrically charged air particles are quickly grounded to the earth when humidity is high, it may not have been the amount of oxygen in the air, but rather the massive ion depletion that caused the adverse effect. The woman moved to a rural community in northern California and cured her respiratory problems.

Another natural situation that results in drastically reduced neg-ions is a high pollen count in the air. Like the dust particles dispersed by the foehn winds, the pollen attracts neg-ions and renders them useless to humans. Thus, people with allergies not only suffer from the effect of the pollen they breathe, but they also must endure the effects caused by the lack of neg-ions.

A good percentage of Europeans use specially built neg-ion generators in their automobiles. In 1965, Mercedes-Benz pioneered research tests to explore the microenvironment of cars in relation to ions. Another major auto/ion exploration was conducted by state-employed scientists in 1972 in Budapest, Hungary. The conclusion was that people in automobiles are overdosed with positive ions in much the same way as those working in modern office buildings. Numerous adverse effects potentially exist, such as drowsiness or irritability. Coordination is reduced, and there is a marked decrease in concentration. The longer a person is in the car, the worse it becomes. One group of scientists reported that their attentiveness is curtailed after spending three hours in positively ionized air.

Certain sections of a city or industrialized area are apt to have lower counts of negatively ionized air. This increases the car accident potential for anyone driving through those areas. It is advisable to roll down the window of the car every few minutes to allow fresh air to come in naturally, instead of using the vents or heater/air-conditioning system, which further deplete the already low supply of negative ions.

There is a point worth mentioning for those who are extremely ion sensitive. A British doctor who specializes in migraine headaches has found that this problem, along with many respiratory ailments, can be associated with an insufficient neg-ion count. Those suffering are advised to wear natural fabrics instead of synthetics, since natural fabrics attract the positive ions before they can be inhaled. Sufferers are also advised to avoid environments in which synthetics, metals, and plastics are widespread.

To summarize the ion effect: An excess of negatively charged ions in the atmosphere will lead to a feeling of exhilaration. An excess of positively charged ions will induce drowsiness, depression, or worse. There is much research yet to be conducted in this area, but even with our present understanding, ions should be considered a major unseen influence for a high percentage of the population.

Chapter 10

PROGRAMMING DREAMS

To understand the effectiveness of dream programming as an unseen influence, you must first understand the subconscious mind and how it works. The subconscious mind is the storehouse for all of your experiences and viewpoints; thus, it is the subconscious that we work with in positive programming and reprogramming. I want you to think of yourself as a mind, as this in reality is what you are. You do not have a mind—you are mind. You are the sum total of all your experiences from the time of your birth up until the present moment. If you believe in reincarnation, then you see that all the experiences of your past lives would be included in your present self.

Regardless of your belief system, these past experiences represent your programming, and memories of them are retained in the subconscious memory banks. Your subconscious mind has made you what you are today. Your talents and abilities, your problems and afflictions are the results of the intuitive guidance of the subconscious. It has been directing you, and it will continue to direct you—often in opposition to your conscious desires.

Why? Because the subconscious has little or no reasoning power. It is simply operating like a computer, functioning as the result of programming. It will help bring into actuality the reality for which it is programmed. If the subconscious were to receive no new programming, it would continue to operate on all of its previous programming. This, of course, cannot happen, for you are constantly feeding it new data. Every thought programs the computer. Thus, if you think negatively, you are programming your computer in the wrong way. You create your own reality with your thoughts.

Many people have no idea how often they think negatively. If you climb out of bed cursing the alarm clock, grouch through breakfast, complain about the rain and the heavy traffic on the freeway, worry about how you dislike your job, and so on throughout the day, you are creating a more negative reality for yourself. Because you are thinking more negative thoughts than positive during the day, there is simply no way you can be creating anything but a negative reality. With all the negative programming of your computer, it can't do anything but create the programmed result: more negativity.

Your thoughts from the past have created your "today." If you don't like your today and desire to change it, it is time to change your programming—your input to the subconscious computer. What your mind has created, your mind can change.

So that you can better understand the importance of these concepts, I'd like to give you a little background from the brain research laboratories and some of the university studies that have been conducted.

Remember: the subconscious programs us. It doesn't reason, but it does work to create the reality according to the programming it is fed. Although this is normally accomplished through thoughts and our life experiences, the brain researchers found that the subconscious is incapable of telling the difference between reality and fantasy, between the real experience and the imagined experience.

One of the initial tests that proved this was the recording of actual brain-wave patterns under specific conditions. Test subjects were placed in a room and wired to an EEG machine. Then one volunteer ran into the room and fired a gun. Someone else danced, a dog barked, a color was projected, and other test situations were created. As the test subjects were exposed to each situation, it caused their brain waves to form patterns on the recording instruments. Each situation was marked on the recording paper so the researchers would know what had transpired in order to create each pattern. "Dog barked here," for example, marked the pattern corresponding to this event.

The next step of the test was to have the subject sit and concentrate upon situations described by the researchers. For example, a researcher might say: "I now want you to imagine yourself watching a woman doing a dance. See it in your mind, fantasize about it, conceive of it with as much imagination as possible. (Pause) All right, I now want you to imagine a dog barking."

While the subject was concentrating upon these imagined situations, his brain waves were once again being recorded. The results of the tests showed that the exact same patterns of up and down brain waves were created when the woman came into the room and did a dance as when the subject imagined her doing a dance. The same was true with all other situations and with all of the test subjects. The brain waves were identical, so the computer part of the brain was obviously incapable of telling the real from the imagined.

Another supportive series of tests was conducted by the University of Chicago. These and many similar tests show how our subconscious computer actually creates the reality for which it is programmed. Three test groups of students took part in a mental programming experiment based upon shooting basketball. All the participating students were tested for their individual basket-shooting ability, and the results were recorded.

Group One was told: "Don't play any basketball for a month. In fact, just forget about basketball for the entire month."

Group Two was told: "You are each to practice shooting baskets for one full hour a day, every day for the month."

Group Three was told: "You are to spend one hour a day imagining you are successfully shooting baskets. Do this every day for the month. Imagine or fantasize yourself as being successful shooting baskets. See every detail of your accomplishments in your mind."

One month later, the three groups were again tested for their ability to shoot baskets. The students in Group One, who hadn't played basketball for a month, tested exactly the same as they did the first time. Those in Group Two, who had been practicing a full hour a day for a month, tested 24% improved in their basket-shooting ability. The Group Three students, who had only imagined they were successfully shooting baskets for an hour a day, tested 23% improved in their actual basket-shooting ability. Only one percentage point less than the group that had actually been practicing!

Obviously, the group that only imagined shooting baskets programmed their subconscious computer to perform almost as effectively as those who actually practiced. The subconscious can be fooled. It can be tricked. It can be programmed, and you simply have to know how to become an effective programmer.

Since we program our lives with our thoughts, imaginings, and fantasies, each of our thoughts is extremely important. Anyone who believes this information and continues to dwell on any form of negativity is foolish beyond words. You can train yourself to recognize adverse thoughts the moment they come into your mind and transform them immediately into positive opportunities. I often advise people to send "love" into their negative thoughts and thus reverse the programming.

"But what about our dreams? Do they fall into the category of imagination and fantasy? After all, we can't control our dreams, and sometimes they're very negative." I've heard this question often from seminar participants. My response is, yes, dreams do program your subconscious, and thus, they become an important factor in the creation of your reality; but no, I do not agree that you can't control them.

Camila Daren was a working wife in her mid-twenties, and as a talented, enthusiastic copywriter, she was rewarded with several promotions during the three years she worked for a local advertising agency. When the creative director of the agency resigned to accept a position elsewhere, Camila was offered his job. She accepted it but privately felt incapable of living up to tripled responsibilities. In an attempt to override these fears, she pushed herself night and day, until she finally began to resent home responsibilities such as cooking and cleaning.

"I was a star at the office but a flop at home," she explained. "There was no time for social activities, and as I look back on it, I don't know how John put up with me, even in the early stages. I couldn't say what I wanted to say at the office, for fear of offending a superior or a client, so I held it all inside until I got home, and I know I took it out on my husband.

"Then the dreams began. They occurred just once in a while at first, but over the weeks it got to the point where every week I'd have three or four bad dreams about John. They were horrible. He was always doing something to hurt me or acting weird in the dreams. I'd wake up in the morning and look at him lying there beside me. I'd just want to hit him in the face. There are many emotions of fear and hatred in dreams, and they don't shut off the moment you open your eyes. The more I had the dreams, the more I seemed to turn off towards him. Little things that had never bothered me, like the cap being left off the toothpaste, became real festering irritations."

Camila continued in her position of creative director for a year after her divorce until she suffered a near nervous breakdown. At this time, her doctor advised her to resign and take a long vacation. She did. I met her several months later when she was seeking to learn self-hypnosis as a tension-alleviation technique.

"Did the nightmares about John continue after you parted?" I asked.

"For a while, but then they switched to my boss or to whichever client was giving me the hardest time at the moment. I know I'm to blame for allowing my job to come before my marriage, but I swear it was the

94

dreams that accelerated our breakup more than anything else."

If emotionless thoughts about shooting a basketball into a basket can successfully program performance, there is little doubt that emotion-packed dreams of fear and hate can also program reality. Camila would have been wise to have altered her dreams before they altered her life.

Ray Willis's case was somewhat different. He and I met through our mutual interest in the martial arts. As Ray explains: "We all have a passive and a violent side to our personalities. In today's society, there are few healthy opportunities to express the violent side, yet if it isn't released in one way, it will come out in another. Athletics is a good way to express this need, but I didn't realize this for a long time. Instead, I lived a sedentary office life-style, smiling and acting cordial whether I felt like it or not. The only time I ever raised my voice was in a fight with my wife and to keep the kids in line, and that wasn't very often because it's self-destructive. Anyway, I had these violent dreams often. Sometimes I'd be using guns, sometimes just beating the hell out of someone, but they happened every few days. I'd awaken in the morning feeling aggressive towards the world, and I'm sure this attitude was often perceived by those around me. Once I started studying martial arts, the violent dreams stopped. I guess harmlessly kicking a punching bag is enough to release these pressures."

It is hard to imagine that working with a punching bag or sparring with another student could program the subconscious in any way other than developing an individual's ability in karate and providing the positive benefits of self-confidence and self-esteem. Yet, it seems to stop violence in dreams. I have talked with others who have experienced situations similar to Ray's. These people alleviated violent dreams through activities such as bike riding, running, and weight lifting.

Although research laboratories all over the world are studying sleep and dreams, we have improved only our technical understanding of what transpires during the five to nine hours of regeneration we all require. Approximately 20,000 volunteers have slept in sleep lab bedrooms, wired to electroencephalograph machines for as little as a few nights or as long as fifty nights. We understand the rapid eye movements and the blood pressure, pulse, temperature, and muscle tension changes that transpire as we move through various levels of consciousness, but we know little about our need of dreams. We have learned that every human being has dreams occurring during REM sleep and that they come at regular intervals of 85 to 110 minutes. This indicates about four or five episodes per night, which add up to about an hour and a half of dreaming. They can be in color or black and white. Some occur in a split second, while others take longer. People deprived of REM sleep have been found to have long dreams with individual episodes lasting up to eighty minutes. When deprived of food and drink, it is common to dream of food and drink. Those leading mundane lives will often have wild dreams, while those leading exhilarating or physically active lives are more likely to dream of calm situations.

The thoughts you have when you fall asleep will often become interwoven into your dreams. I remembered a good example of this in the middle of writing this chapter. Trenna and I often read in bed before going to sleep. She had fallen asleep early while reading an occult thriller and two hours later began to talk in a disturbed tone. I awakened her, and she explained she was reliving one of the horrifying incidents in the book but replaced some of the characters with real personalities who are friends and associates.

To retire immediately after watching the evening news would seem unwise for the same reason. The same is true of crossing over into sleep while dwelling upon a negative situation in your life, or after a fight with your spouse. You will intensify your negative programming at this time. Advocates of sleep learning would have you fall asleep listening to positive programming. They know it is an effective conditioning technique. In going to sleep, you move from the con-

Section II

THE METAPHYSICAL INFLUENCES

Chapter 11

METAPHYSICAL POTENTIALS

The occasion was a three-day psychic seminar on re-programming your life. It was noon of the second day. I had just completed a lengthy lecture on unseen influences, and most of the participants were filing out of the room while I shut down the audio board and began to cue a videotape for afternoon projection.

"The situation you were just talking about, Dick, could have been mine."

A pretty brown-haired woman of about twenty-eight had come up on stage. "I'm in the middle of an affair that is going nowhere," she continued, "and my entire life seems to be coming apart at the seams."

All seminar participants are required to wear name tags to indicate who belongs in the sessions and so I can keep conversation on a first-name basis without attempting to memorize names. Her name tag identified her as Elaine Hurley from Milwaukee, Wisconsin.

"Elaine," I said with a smile and nodded in acknowledgment but continued to work.

"Could I talk to you, please? I'm only going to be here in Arizona for the three days of the seminar, and I really feel that you could help me. I know you're doing that in these sessions, but I'd like to follow up on what you just talked about."

I had noticed her in the audience. She was very pretty, but had sad brown eyes. She was one of those who listened to every word of the seminar, in addition to recording it all on cassettes. "Sure. I'm to meet Trenna in the hotel dining room for lunch in about fifteen minutes. Why don't you join us there, unless you have other plans?"

"Fine, that would be fine. I'll see you in a few minutes."

Trenna and Elaine were already talking at the table when I arrived. "Elaine and I just discovered that we were both born in Twin Falls, Idaho, and only six months apart," Trenna said as I sat down.

"How do you feel it went this morning?" I asked.

"Fine, from what I observed," Trenna replied. "But I had to be in and out of the room to cover some details on late registrations. This is really a serious group, isn't it?"

"Aren't they always serious?" Elaine asked.

"To a degree, but it does vary. Some groups are lighter. Others are down-to-business. The astrologers whom we work with to plan the dates have accurately described the mood of the last ten gigs weeks in advance, and all by mathematically plotting the stars," I explained.

"Well, that is part of the reason I wanted to talk with you. I hadn't planned to have an astrologer do my chart or investigate any of the other psychic areas, but I wonder if I should. You mentioned that any of these unseen influences could be affecting us right now." She flipped open a note pad and read them back to me. "I want to find out what I'm up against—what forces have created the messed-up life I'm now living."

"Elaine, I consider those influences to be what most people call destiny. I don't want to get ahead of tomorrow's sessions and lectures, but I will tell you that you control your own destiny to the degree that you evolve a self-actualized perspective and live a sensible life-style. At that point, you rise above such effects. Of course, there are very few people who have the nutritional/physical discipline to achieve this perspective completely, but every little bit helps. Most people

101

simply go through life as victims of destiny, not realizing that they are responsible for what happens to them."

"Why don't you give us some background on your present situation?" Trenna suggested.

"Okay. I have two children and was divorced a little over a year ago. It seems that for the last several years nothing has gone right in my life. I'm presently working as a home mortgage loan closer in a Milwaukee savings and loan, and the job is boring and miserable. John is a man I've been seeing for over six months, and our relationship seems to be going nowhere. One day I feel the strength to tell him we're through, but then the insecurity sets in, and I don't do it. My parents live a couple of miles from me, and they are constantly telling me how horribly I'm raising Peggy and David, my children. My mother comes by on Sundays and takes David to church service, which he hates, and the result is a huge scene every week. Today is Sunday, isn't it? Yes, you know, this is the first Sunday in almost a year that I haven't dreaded.

"Anyway, I see no signs of a desirable future," she continued. "I can go on like this forever, I suppose, but what a dreadful thought. I want to change it all. That's why I came to the seminar."

"All we can do is expose you to some concepts that could help you help yourself," Trenna explained. "There is no magic wand. Yet, these concepts often seem to help people understand why they have the problems."

"But that isn't necessary," I added. "The self can be created according to your own specifications. What about your marriage, Elaine? Can you sum up the problems?"

"I can sum it up by saying I was often beaten," she said. "We argued and fought and slowly grew apart over the seven years we were together, but it was his increasing violence that triggered the divorce. It was never directed at the children, just at me."

"Did he want the divorce, too?"

"Not really, but he accepted it easily enough. After it was over, he beat me up once when he came to see

102

the kids. I called the police and had him arrested. Since then, he comes by to see the kids once in a while, but he says no more than is necessary to me. He just stares at me with hatred in his eyes."

"Delightful atmosphere you live in. What does he do for a living?" I asked.

"Don is a stockbroker. Hardly the type, huh? Would you advise that I see one of the astrologers while I'm here?" she asked.

"If you feel the need," I replied. "Tell her nothing, except that you would like her to investigate the last couple of years and provide you with some positive advice and direction for the future. See what happens."

"Has anyone requested to be part of the chakra link this afternoon, Richard?" Trenna asked.

"Not to me."

"Then why don't I do a hookup with you, Elaine? If you'd like to participate, it might provide information."

In some of our early seminars, Trenna used her unique abilities to mentally connect the top three energy points of her body, the chakras, with those of another person. With the aid of a deeply induced hypnotic trance, she can relive the subject's past and often provide extremely accurate information about his or her present.

Her technique has been described by Brad Steiger, the prolific author of books on the psychic world, reincarnation, and UFOs. Brad first observed Trenna's work when he toured several cities with us in 1977. After the tour, Brad and his family moved to Scottsdale, and we became personal friends. In his book, *You Will Live Again* (Dell: April, 1978), he describes Trenna's skill.

Trenna Sutphen works in many ways during the past-life seminars, but probably the most dramatic is her ability to perceive the past lives of others and then provide them with present-life psychic information from the higher self hypnotic levels.

103

For a chakra hookup demonstration in each seminar, a volunteer is chosen from the participants. Trenna now lies in a lounger on the stage while the subject sits beside her in a chair. Dick begins to hypnotize her and, as part of the induction, completes an elaborate set of instructions which connect the top three energy chakras of the two people.

A very real "psychic link" is now established, and Dick usually induces an even deeper trance.

When this is complete, he instructs Trenna to draw upon the connecting link and allow the memories from the subject's subconscious mind to flow into her own. She is now instructed to begin to relive a portion of a past life that would be of value for the volunteer subject to know of in the present.

When the group of ninety people reassembled in the ballroom, the seminar host introduced a videotape of a panel discussion on reincarnation.

The chakra-link demonstration was next on the schedule, and when the videotape was over, a recliner lounge chair was brought onto the small stage. Trenna took her place on it and Elaine sat on one side, while I took my place on the other. A microphone was positioned close to Trenna's lips, and the room was darkened, with only one light illuminating the stage area. While Trenna began her deep breathing, I explained the procedure to the audience.

The process begins with instructions to relax the body and mind. The chakra link is made, and the hypnotic induction completed.

"All right, Trenna, you have the power and ability to draw upon the chakra connection with Elaine. We are searching for past-life information that would relate to the situations she has experienced with her ex-husband Don in this life. If the two of them have been together before, I want you to move in time to an important situation that transpired in another time and another place. So, let's let go now . . . draw upon the connection . . . I will count backward from three to one. On the count of one, very vivid impressions will come into your mind, and you will speak up and communicate what you can perceive. Number three, moving backward in time now . . . feel it happening . . . number two . . . allow it to happen . . . you are moving back to an important or clarifying situation in one of Elaine's prior lifetimes . . . number one . . . you are now there. Allow the impressions to come into focus. Then speak up and tell me what is transpiring."

Trenna was quiet, REMs active, indicating a deep trance. A minute passed, and she spoke. "Y'all act like low-borns!" The voice had a thick Southern drawl. Trenna wasn't just observing Elaine's prior life. She had become the person and was *reliving* an event from the past.

"Who the hell ya think ya are?" she yelled out, snapping her head and almost knocking the microphone out of the stand. Elaine jumped.

"What is happening?" I asked softly.

"Oh, I was just funnin' Tommy and Leslie. They was tryin' to steal some extra nibbles. But their plates're full, and they eatin' over on the dough bench now."

Q. So, you're a cook, is that correct?
A. Sure, sure.
Q. What is your name?
A. Bessie . . . ole' Bessie. (She laughs to herself. Trenna weighs about one hundred and twenty pounds, but she now sways in the chair as if she weighed two hundred.)
Q. Where do you live, Bessie?
A. One half a day ride from 'Lanta.
Q. Atlanta, Georgia?
A. I said that.
Q. Is there anything special about today, Bessie?
A. Nah . . . don't think so. Just like all the other days 'round here. There is a wagon comin' in at break-a-leg speed.
Q. Tell me what is happening.

A. Oh, Lawdy . . . oh, Lawdy . . . da whites done killed Jasper . . . da whites done killed Emmer . . . oh, no . . . oh, no . . . Jimmy Bellows is running in here to hide . . . oh, no he don't . . . oh, no he don't do that.

Q. Who is Jimmy Bellows?

A. Master's cousin from 'Lanta . . . he crazy . . . he twitch and act crazy. He killed Jasper and Emmer. WHAT YOU DO, JIMMY BELLOWS? WHAT YOU DO? YOU CAN'T JUST GO KILLIN' BLACK FOLK LIKE THAT! NO! NO! I WON'T!

Q. What is he doing, Bessie?

A. Tryin' to hide in here. I'll fix his . . . ah . . . grah . . . oh . . . ah . . . ! (Trenna is jerking in the chair, and her face is contorted and angry.)

Q. I want to know what is happening.

A. I hit 'im with the hot poker from the fire. Smells bad . . . he a-screamin' and twitchin', and the black folk got 'im now . . . they pullin' off his pants . . . oh, Lawdy . . . he a-yellin' at me . . . oh, Lawdy . . . Tim is . . . oh, no! (Her voice is very anguished, so I remove her from the scene.)

Q. All right, let's let go of this now. I want you to let go of everything that has transpired and return to the present time, remembering everything, but on the count of three, you'll be back in the present, remaining in a deep, deep, hypnotic sleep. One . . . two . . . three. You are now here, and I want you to breathe deeply and relax completely. That's it . . . all right now, Trenna, I want you to move up into the higher self mental levels of your mind, still drawing upon the chakra link with Elaine. Let's begin to transcend into the all-knowing mental realms. (Instructions given.) I now want you to allow any information that would be of value to Elaine to be verbalized. If her own masters or guides can impart any information to you, that would be fine . . . anything that you can perceive . . . let it come in.

A. (Trenna now speaks in her own soft voice.) Jimmy Bellows is Don Hurley in this life. The blacks let

106

him die slowly, and all the while he was directing his animosity at Bessie, whom he felt could have hidden him but instead was the direct cause of his capture and its results. Such a tie can span centuries. Don felt that he was ready to let go of the old hatred, so in this life he tested his evolvement by becoming involved with Elaine. Obviously, he hasn't yet learned that love—not hatred and violence—is the answer. Elaine agreed to coexplore this situation with him before either of them were born. By opening herself to it, she was balancing a situation from an Egyptian incarnation that did not involve Don. Let me see . . . Elaine is very warm to the black cause in this life . . . in fact, I believe she has been actively involved in helping them in this life.

I looked at Elaine. She shook her head in agreement with the statement.
Trenna continued:

There is something more here. It's important, but I can't quite . . . ah . . . Don is very sensitive psychically. He doesn't realize it . . . in fact, he doesn't even like to talk about psychic things, but he says that he is a "good guesser." There is something about the house you live in . . . it is a brick rambler style, and you moved there about three years ago . . . and it was then that the trouble erupted. Don was being tested . . . no . . . I don't know. Oh . . . I see an old man, and he is fighting with his wife . . . really fighting and yelling. They never stop fighting. She eventually dies, and a couple years later so does he. It seems that even after her death, the wife returns to mentally harass him. He died in that house and they or their energy is still there. Don psychically perceives that energy and absorbs it himself. It contributes to his violent nature.

Q. Is there anything more you can relate to Elaine?
A. I can see Elaine's mother. She wears blue . . . al-

ways wears blue. (Elaine nods in agreement.) This situation in the past is not important, but Elaine must stand up to this woman in a loving, assertive way. I would highly suggest that she take A.T. (Assertiveness Training) at a local school or college. It is time for Elaine to make some major changes in her life. There are many beautiful things waiting for her, but unless she takes charge of her life and acts in an assertive way, they will fade away. I see a brown-haired man. He has very curly hair, and this relates to what I am receiving.

(End of the chakra-link session)

"Is there anything you can tell us in response to what Trenna told you from the higher self?" I asked Elaine, who was still sitting beside Trenna.

"Well, it all relates to my life. I didn't talk with Trenna about most of those things before this session. I know we bought our house as part of an estate sale, but I don't know anything about the people that lived there before. Trenna is certainly right that it was after we moved in that the trouble really became bad. Of course, I still live there, even though I wish I didn't. Let me see. Yes, I have been very active in trying to help blacks. My best girlfriend in Milwaukee is black. Oh, yes, Don, my ex-husband, is very psychic, although he won't admit it. 'A good guesser' is a direct quote that he often uses."

"What about a guy with curly brown hair?" Trenna asked.

"The only person that could refer to is a man I sat next to on the airplane to Arizona. He lives in Milwaukee but is in the middle of moving out here, transferring his business, I guess. We did exchange phone numbers, and he was really interested in the seminar and reincarnation."

Elaine later had an astrology chart plotted. It predicted upheaval in her life over the two-year period. Marital problems were indicated, and she was completing a major Saturn transit.

The last night of the seminar, all participants met in

Rawhide, a cowboy town on the edge of Scottsdale. We all rode a haywagon out into the desert for a windup banquet. Elaine was sitting alone by the large campfire, and I went over and joined her.

"I don't want to go back home," she said, her big brown eyes sadder than ever. "This place—this town and valley—has to be the greatest I've ever been." She was holding a cup of coffee in one hand and gesturing to the surrounding mountains with the other.

"Why not move here, Elaine?"

"How could I do that? It's a nice area, and I'm sick of the snow and cold and my general environment. But that environment is security for me."

"If you really wanted to move here, you would. Security doesn't mean anything. You are your own security. I hear people say 'I wish I could' all the time, but they don't really mean it. They are more secure in their insecurity, simply because it is familiar."

"I don't even know if I could get a job out here," she said.

My response was a disapproving look.

"Well, I'm sure I could find something. Do you suppose they need home loan closers in Arizona?"

"There are probably three times as many houses being built here due to the Sun Belt migration. People fear change, Elaine. You can do anything you desire to do. It is simply a matter of reevaluation."

Three months later, Elaine walked into my office, accompanied by a man with curly brown hair. "Dick, I want you to meet John Amara. You probably don't remember, but I told you I'd met someone like Trenna described on the airplane to Arizona."

"Elaine, I have a very good memory for pretty girls with sad brown eyes," I said, shaking hands with John. "And your eyes aren't sad anymore."

"When I got back to Milwaukee, I investigated the background of the house. It was exactly as Trenna described. I was so happy in Arizona, and back home it was 'depression city' all over again. So, I decided to make a right-angle turn and move to Phoenix. I sold the house, and the day before I was to leave, John called to ask me out to dinner."

The three of us had lunch together, and I learned more about the unseen influences affecting Elaine.

Elaine: "The ESP mind-projection tests we did at the seminar showed me that I was psychic myself. When I got home, I sat back and listened to the tapes I'd recorded here, and I went over a checklist of the unseen influences. Of the fifteen, there is no doubt that eleven, and maybe more, were affecting me all at once.

"My mother draws off my energy, even over a tele-phone line, so the vitality vampirism was most apropos. My work environment in the savings and loan was cer-tainly a situation of psychic attack caused by negative thoughts of other people around me. Five of us had originally applied for my position. After I got it, the other four acted jealously toward me. In reference to dream programming, I recalled how often I'd awaken remembering a bad dream about my ex-husband."

John: "Tell him about the parallel-life situation, Elaine."

Elaine: "Oh, yes. When we did the parallel trans-ference session at the seminar, I received information on a woman living in Guatemala. Now, that isn't some-place I'm familiar with. In fact, I didn't know if it was on this continent or over in Africa. I picked up on a time period a couple of years prior to the session, and the woman lived near a lake called something similar to 'Elizabeth.' I couldn't even pronounce the woman's name, so naturally there would be no way for me to find her. The situation was one of tremendous sadness, because she had recently lost her child in a flood. A little research showed me that there is a huge lake in Guatemala called 'Izabal.' And to top it off, there was flooding in that area a couple of years ago."

Dick: "So, if that woman is another aspect of your soul, you were superconsciously perceiving her emo-tions, and they were filtering down into your consciousness in the form of a depression you assumed stemmed solely from your immediate environment."

Once you understand the degree of external manipulation, you will want to improve your life—to cut the puppet strings and walk away. I explain the influences and how people can rise above them, but that's all. You must take it upon yourself to use the knowledge to change your life.

Chapter 12

PAST AND PARALLEL LIVES

"Oh, come on, Dick, what you did in your past life dictates all the situations you find yourself experiencing now. That's karma, and you don't need to go into all of these unseen influences. If you understand your past, it explains your present. If you handle things correctly in this life, you'll have an easier time in your next life!"

How often I have heard such statements following an appeal to reason and a lecture on unseen influences. Yet, after years of researching reincarnation, writing books on the subject, and regressing countless numbers of people, I do not accept this fatalistic thinking.

Either you learned in the past that certain foods promoted health while others were degenerative, or you didn't learn that information and are suffering or will suffer the consequences. You learned in the past to listen to your own body rhythms. If not, the consequences show up in the way that you now function. There are certainly good examples of cause and effect, or karma, if you prefer. I, however, don't view karma as a mystical concept. It is simple logic and easily explained medically.

The chapter on programming dreams explains how your subconscious is programmed by your thoughts. The subconscious doesn't reason; it acts according to input from you in order to create the reality for which it is programmed. The result is much the same as a computer. Karma is nothing but the past input to your computer—input from your past lives and from your present life up until now. "Parallels," "separate selves" or "counterparts" are terms used to communicate the simultaneous, multiple incarnation of various physical entities of the same oversoul. These entities are all living on the earth plane at the same time, overlapping in physical manifestation.

In other words, you may also be someone else. Assuming you are a California housewife, your oversoul might also have been incarnated as a male farmer in Russia, a female restaurant cook in Denmark, and a teenage boy in South America. You are superconsciously in communication with your parallels at all times, but you are consciously unaware of this communication. The abilities of these counterparts may be influencing you. For example, you may have a green thumb when it comes to raising houseplants, or you're known to your peer group as a gourmet cook. The South American teenager has a natural ear for music and learned to play the guitar several years ago, so when you decided to learn guitar three months ago, you learned easily. You perceived intuitively from your parallel who already knew how to play the guitar. The fact that you were raised riding horses may prove to be an advantage to him should he ever decide to take up the sport. The Danish cook went through a painful divorce last year, and you experienced the feeling that everything just wasn't right for several months.

Part of my last book, *Past Lives, Future Loves,* is devoted to the concept of parallel lives and the evidence and patterns I collected in working with people all over the country. Since writing that book, we have heard from many other people who have explored their parallel potentials in a seminar or a taped hypnosis session and then followed up on the information they received.

A woman who attended our annual seven-day seminar in the summer of 1977 returned to the 1978 sessions and explained her experience to all participants. While lying on the darkened ballroom floor of the

113

Mountain Shadows Resort during the parallel transfer session, participants were given the following instructions: "You feel completely relaxed and at ease, and we are now going to work together to see if we can establish a connection between you and another individual who is also you. Your soul or oversoul may be exploring more than one life at this time on the earth, or perhaps you have had a parallel who has already crossed over into spirit but had lived at some time during your present life.

"If you are currently experiencing a lifetime in another's physical body, your own superconscious mind is fully aware of this fact. Your higher self is aware of everything that relates to you. If you do have or have had a parallel self, you have the power and ability to allow a mental transference to take place, and you will see this other identity as an emotionless observer would see it. You will tap in on some part of its life, and the situation will be either a positive, neutral, or a happy one. You may see things through its eyes, or you may find yourself observing it." Additional transfer instructions were provided, and once completed, the participants were given time to observe the mental visualizations. Next, questions were asked which the participants sought to answer in their minds using their observations in hypnosis. Some participants were able to move in time, thus learning detailed information about their other self. There were many exacting questions, such as the full name of the parallel, addresses, family information, et cetera.

The woman from the 1977 session described her experience. "I saw myself as a woman living on a hillside on the outskirts of Kingston, Jamaica. I had four children and lived in a small house that I could see very vividly. Although I received a name and an address, I didn't know how to spell them, so I couldn't contact her by mail. It was all so very real that I couldn't forget it after the session. I had additional vacation time coming, so I decided to go to Kingston and see if I could find her. Although it took a few days, I did find her, and the situation was exactly as I'd observed it—

the children, the house, everything. I ended up staying with her for a week, and I don't believe I've ever felt as close to anyone. There were many parallel incidents that we had shared in our lives that added validity to this idea. Even if we aren't parallels, I must be on some kind of wavelength with her to have received so much accurate information from thousands of miles away and from a country I hardly knew existed."

Other people have come face-to-face with supposed parallel selves and had quite the opposite reaction. They didn't get along at all and seemed to be at opposite ends of the spectrum on all subjects. In questioning the seminar participants after group transfer sessions, I have found that about 30% have observed a person who is very much like themselves in one or more ways; affinity ties existed. Fifty percent observed no obvious similarities, and 20% have observed diametrically opposed opposites. The theory here might be the yin/yang concept of counterpart duality, the learning of opposing traits which would result in a more complete understanding by the total soul (oversoul).

Gene Carrico used a prerecorded tape to explore the life of one of his parallel selves. Each time he went into hypnosis and the tape instructed him to make the transfer, he found himself observing a man in his late fifties or early sixties. "Everything centered around his room in a hotel or rooming house in Seattle, Washington," Gene explained to me on the phone. "I'd watch him reading or fixing a can of soup over a little hot plate he kept hidden away. On only two occasions did I see him outside of the room, once shopping for groceries and another time exchanging books at one of those used paperback bookstores. He brought in six and traded them for four different titles—all westerns. The only exacting information I received was in watching him address an envelope. He wrote his name and address in the return address corner, and I remembered it upon awakening. The calendar on the desk was for July, 1967—over ten years prior to the parallel exploration sessions."

Gene explained that he lived in Dallas, Texas, but had a cousin in Seattle. He called his relative requesting him to check on the address. "I wanted to see whether the whole thing was a figment of my imagination or if it had some validity. Well, as it turned out, the address was that of an old hotel that caters to weekly or monthly roomers. I called the hotel, but my parallel didn't live there now. The clerk told me they didn't have records from ten years ago."

During the 1977 and 1978 seminars, before awakening the parallel session participants, I instructed them to go up into their higher minds and asked them how many parallel selves they had. The common numbers were two or three. Four was the highest anyone reported. Using a tape allows an individual unlimited exploration opportunities, and so I decided to call, at random, several people who had purchased a parallel-selves tape. The following is a summary of several of those calls.

Twenty-eight-year-old female secretary: She observed two different parallel situations on many occasions. One person was an English male office worker in his forties. He was married and had three children, all boys. "His life is b-o-r-i-n-g," she told me. The second individual was a much older woman living in what she perceived to be an Arabian country. "She helps take care of her daughter-in-law and one granddaughter. I've never seen her son, so assume he ran off or is dead. I can't understand any of the communication, so I'm not even sure where they live."

Thirty-six-year-old housewife: She observed four different parallel situations the first four times she used the tape. She then continued to experience the same situations, or, on a few occasions, different experiences with the same people. She never received enough direct information to attempt to contact any of her counterparts and wasn't sure she would try anyway. "What would I tell them?" she asked. "Hello there, I'm you, and I'd like to talk to you about it!"

116

Three of the parallel selves were an Asian woman in her late twenties, a ten-year-old boy living in what she thought was New York City, and a black woman in Boston who worked in an insurance office in a secretarial position. "The fourth is also a woman. This is really embarrassing, but she is a prostitute in an Iron Curtain country."

There seemed to be no obvious affinity ties between any of the counterparts, but there was very little information known about them.

Twenty-year-old male college student: He observed one parallel on numerous occasions—a middle-aged European farmer. "His life is quite mundane," he explained, "but he is a happy family man who thoroughly enjoys his work and takes pride in it. My own apartment is filled with plants, and I even have tomatoes and lettuce growing on a little balcony here. I started raising plants in my room at home when I was about nine years old."

Fifty-one-year-old female practical nurse: She observed two parallels several times before becoming bored with them. "I never saw anything very interesting." I explained that the tape is programmed so that she could only observe positive, neutral, or happy situations, but that she could use self-hypnosis to explore anything she wanted. Anyone accustomed to using tapes is already conditioned for self exploration. In response to my question about the parallels, she replied, "Well, one is a young man in California, and all that interests him is chasing girls. The other is a woman close to my own age who, near as I can tell, is only concerned with entertaining her cronies at tea."

"What would you consider interesting enough to warrant further observations?" I asked.

"To see what that young man does with a girl when he finally catches her," she laughed.

Thirty-five-year-old male salesman: He observed two parallels. One was a young man working in a meat-processing plant in the Midwest, and another was a middle-aged woman working as a part-time meteorologist in Florida. "The only affinity tie that I'm aware of is that we are all gourmets and share a weight problem," he explained.

Of the twelve subjects I telephoned, ten had observed parallel situations. One saw only an endless stream of faces moving past him, and the last one had no results at all in using the tape. He did explain that past-life tapes worked very well for him, so he assumed that he had no parallels and gave the tape to a friend who had results similar to the situations I have just described.

Trenna and I have received letters from many people claiming to have had contact with their parallel selves. In one situation, a woman explained that her counterpart looked very much like her, with similar features, hairstyle, tastes, and interests. A man claimed that his counterpart is a female companion and offered impressive evidence to support his claim.

Since there is no way to prove or disprove the concept, I remain on the fence pending further evidence. Again, I return to the unlimited power of the mind as the explanation for an individual who accurately perceives information about an unknown person living thousands of miles away.

Chapter 13

ASTROLOGY

I won't pretend to understand the inner workings of an astrology chart, although I've worked with astrologers for years. I rely upon their knowledge, for the best astrologers have devoted their entire lives to understanding how the planetary movements influence our lives. This craft becomes almost a science in the hands of a true professional. It is through personal experience that I have learned to respect astrological potentials.

Hazel W. Mooney is one of the finest and most responsible astrologers with whom I've had personal contact. Before giving a personal reading or taped session, Hazel makes the following statement:

> The ultimate purpose of astrology is to serve as a guide through your physical life, but the soul must have awakened before the value of the horoscope can be fully appreciated. Self-understanding and destiny—the self must be known, the destiny must be fulfilled; therefore, character is destiny. The birth chart is merely a symbolic representation of potential development. All of the aspects are intended only for learning and are, therefore, benevolent. Since all suffering is the result of ignorance, astrology seeks to answer the question: "Why?" It is a benefit, therefore, to know both the harmonious and inharmonious aspects in your

chart. All fate is the result of thoughts, which are the roots of your character. To know yourself is to become wise and thus, to master fate. Free will is a divine gift to all. As you gain in understanding, you can avoid much of the negative conditioning and use the positive aspects to full enjoyment. The desire to give love and be loved will reach a perfected state in you through many lifetimes of practicing, giving, and understanding love, as it ceases to be personal love and becomes selfless love. So, continue to unfold in love, believe in love, and give of the inner self to love. Eventually you will reach that level where all is expressed and experienced in fullness. If others do not understand your viewpoint of giving warm love to life and do not return it to you in like fashion, pay it no heed, for it does not matter to your own inner awareness whether or not you are understood or loved in return. You are reaching for the ultimacy of all things; and you have to practice and experience for many, many lives before it is finally attained.

Hazel W. Mooney, certified as a professional astrologer by the Astrologers Guild of America and The International School of Astrology, N.Y.C.

Roberta Mueller is one of the country's most respected astrologers, having been featured in two books by Ruth Montgomery and titles by Hans Holzer and Jess Stern. Trenna and I first met Roberta several years ago while conducting a seminar in her hometown of Houston, Texas, where she directs the Magi Astrology Center. Roberta explained that she began studying scientific astrology and setting up charts in 1947. She has been a professional practitioner since 1962.

For inclusion in this book, I asked Roberta to talk with me about astrology as an unseen influence. The following is her simplified explanation.

"The science of astrology is widely misunderstood, even by those who profess to 'believe' in it. (There are millions who 'believe' in it, but who are ignorant of its real workings. There are other millions who 'don't believe' in it, who are equally ignorant of its true nature.)

"Even its classification as a science is open to debate. Call it that, and chances are you will be corrected. When we get right down to it, probably only mathematics could be called a true, pure science. Other disciplines, such as medicine and astrology, are based upon scientific principles. In the case of astrology, mathematical formulae and known astronomical facts are used in the calculating and setting up of the charts. These are functions which can be duplicated over and over again. In medicine, too, scientific principles are utilized when lab tests are run. However, delineation (interpretation) of astrological charts is an art, as in medical diagnosis. True astrology is actually a combination of astronomy, mathematics, philosophy, and psychology.

"Much has been written about the scientific proof of planetary influence. Climate, weather, and oceanic tides are all clearly influenced by sun, moon, and other heavenly bodies. Every living creature—plant, animal, and human—responds to cosmic change. All living things are subject to cycles, and cycles within cycles. It has also been noted that, whatever the length of the cycle—whether three and a half years, nine years, or whatever—all cycles of the same length tend to turn at the same time, acting in synchrony.

"The well-known effects of such phenomena as sunspots can be quite dramatic and clearly observable. When radio, telephone, and telegraph receptions are disrupted, we sit up and take notice. Predicting sunspots and solar flares is a matter of serious interest to scientists at NASA. Dire results might be expected were our astronauts subjected to the dangerous particles and rays thrown out into space by solar flares, once the men were outside the protection of the earth's atmosphere and magnetic field.

"While it is obvious that Earth and other planets are affected by magnetic storms on the sun, conversely, these storms are triggered by the positions of the planets. Mr. John Nelson, retired from RCA, has for years been predicting the timing of these storms, with ninety-four percent accuracy. Sunspots are most frequent when the planets make angles which are multiples of right angles, as seen from the sun (heliocentric astrology).

"On a personal basis, we are affected by the planetary activity and alignments. The birth chart appears to be the pattern of destiny, the key to personality, character, vocation, aptitudes, and psychological make-up. Accepting reincarnation as a cycle of learning, astrology is a symbolic picture of the lessons you came back to learn—the rough edges that could stand a bit of polishing. The natal chart indicates the overall pattern—your abilities, your psychological assets and liabilities, the trend your life is apt to take.

"The progressed chart is generally done for the coming twelve months and is the timer indicating lessons and opportunities for that particular time period. Even novices and students can make general predictions from the progressions and transits. (No reputable astrologer makes predictions based upon transits alone or takes one or two aspects out of context with the rest of the pattern.) The more experienced astrologer with a knowledge of all the various factors, such as fixed stars and asteroids, as well as planets, may see the finer details of the client's life to an astounding degree.

"An adverse progression between Moon and Mars, for instance, often indicates a period of accident-proneness coming up. What kind of accident? It's easy to assume an auto mishap, but this isn't necessarily so. One can slip in the bathtub, fall downstairs, walk through a glass door, slide down the hall on junior's skate, cut a finger while slicing cheese, burn one's fingers taking a roast from the oven, or a strange dog may decide to taste you. The astrologer must often walk a tightrope. If we fail to warn of coming danger, we have failed in our duty. But at the same time, we must be careful not to frighten, and above all, not to program negativity."

Roberta goes on to explain an experience from early

childhood that convinced her of the validity of astrology: "In order to prove that my mother's accurate astrological predictions were all 'coincidence,' I set up charts for certain memorable years in the past. In each case, it was like reading a diary—every important event that had happened was indicated in the chart for that particular year.

"What really capped the bottle was that I have Mars in my chart conjunct the fixed star Dorsum, which, according to the books, gives 'danger of bites from venomous creatures.' The star Altair, on my Midheaven, gives 'danger from reptiles.' Progressed Moon conjoined Mars, and of course, Dorsum, soon after my sixth birthday, and opposed Neptune in Leo, which rules the back. That summer, heavy transits touched off the progressions, and I was bitten by a copperhead snake on my back between the shoulderblades. At that time, neither the snake nor I knew anything about astrology; so certainly, no one 'programmed' us—and ignorance did not keep it from happening."

I asked Roberta how unseen astrological influences were affecting people she had worked with, and how she helped them. She replied: "A dentist brings his patients' birth data, and the writer does the charts, without ever seeing the patients. We tape the analysis, with general health indications and psychological make-up from the natal chart and coming trends from the progressed chart. If chiropractic adjustments seem to be indicated, the chart will generally indicate which vertebrae are out of alignment. We make out the list and send the patient to the chiropractor of his or her choice. In most cases, the list agrees with the chiropractor's subsequent X rays and examination. (Perhaps someday fewer X rays, hence less unnecessary radiation, will be used as other methods of seeing into the body become perfected.) This enlightened dentist believes in holistic health and aims at improving dental health through improving the general health of the body, in addition to relieving the immediate dental problems.

"Naturally, financial trends also are indicated in the

progressed chart. An interesting recent case is that of a lady oil driller who came to me this past June [1978] for a reevaluation of her chart. I had told her two years previously to hold on to a certain piece of property, as it would turn out to be extremely valuable. She did; now she wanted to begin drilling operations for a gas well. The progressed chart for this year indicated that the time was right; she and her partner could not miss. There were several other investors, and most of them came to have their charts evaluated, also. All the charts showed gain through oil and/or gas. As someone pointed out, surely this would not work unless the oil or gas were there in the first place. True—the partner in the venture is an excellent geologist, and he knew where to drill. The charts of the investors and operators and an elective chart for the well itself indicated when drilling should begin. Had the charts of the investors shown a loss through the oil and gas, the obvious conclusion would have been that it was a dry hole and drilling should have, in that case, been postponed. Even in a proven field, one can get a 'duster.' We can do the right thing, but if it's the wrong time, we've still blown it. Basically, this is the name of the game: astrology is the science of timing.

"Next, a chart was erected for the time and date that the well was spudded. It indicated a great gas well, and that's what we got. Earlier in the year, before the operators had consulted me, they had drilled another well close to the new one. It should have been a good well also, but something went wrong in the completion, and it had to be shut in. They had 'shot' or perforated the well when Mercury was retrograde—and that's a no-no! Half of what we do under a retrograde Mercury has to be done over; so it may be that this previous well will be completed at a later date. Let's hope it's when Mercury is direct!"

The question of predestination is a never-ending debate among metaphysically oriented people. I asked Roberta how she felt about this concept as it related to an astrology chart.

"Some events seem so fated they are almost bound

to occur, no matter what; but usually, they can be mitigated considerably. We all have free will. Some people seem to have more self-determination than others and are more in control of their own destiny.

"If an event is seemingly unavoidable, one might as well plan around that event and make the best of it. For over a year, my husband has urged me to get rid of my car and buy a new one. A look at my progressed chart indicated that I was going to have some expensive car trouble from time to time during 1978, regardless of whether I had a new or old vehicle. So, I decided to wait. Besides, as I had told him over a year ago, my car would be wiped out in October, 1978, and I'd much prefer it happened to the old car that I was ready to get rid of anyway. I would buy a new one after October, 1978—not before. Well, he reasoned, why don't I just drive carefully?

" 'Jim,' I said, 'that aspect in early October is so exact, it doesn't much matter what I'm doing or not doing. Someone could jump the curb and hit it in my own parking lot. I'm doing no driving in early October.'

"Well, would you believe? On October 5, 1978, I was at my desk talking to a client, when we heard what sounded like a clap of thunder. (It was raining.) Next, there was a knock at the door, and a neighbor asked, 'I guess that was your car?'

"Sure enough, a young man driving a truck had hit a slick spot, lost control, jumped the curb, hit my car and totaled it, hit another truck and totaled that, then hit a brick planter and leveled it. Miraculously, no one was injured.

"If you know your chart, you just don't get many surprises, unless you have overlooked something."

Barbara Phillips is an astrologer from Tucson, Arizona, who has worked with Trenna and me at many seminars. Her friendly personality and down-to-earth explanations of astrological concepts have helped many novices to understand this unseen effect upon their lives. Her personal investigations of new astrological potentials are always of interest to me. I recently asked her what specialty she was exploring. She agreed with

Roberta's statement that more and more psychologists are astrologers, and she went on to explain: "I'm now examining astrological psychological profiles as a particular significance in the treatment of mental disorders and potential mental disorders which may arise later in life. For example, I am finding in the birth charts of diagnosed schizophrenics certain common denominators which are always present. Since schizophrenia is usually diagnosed later in life, perhaps there are some things we can do to prevent it from occurring if the indicators of the potential for affliction are discovered in early life. I have come to some conclusions along this line regarding the early childhood environment—including diet, sound, color, and texture—which may be helpful to the child with the potential in his chart.

"For the average individual, the astrological psychological profile can be helpful in understanding such things as attitudes towards the opposite sex and how to deal with them; psychoses of various types; self-image; guilt feelings and how to handle guilt; assertiveness, aggressiveness, or the lack of those characteristics; and much more."

Such knowledge obviously can be of great benefit to mankind, but how far should we trust astrology? As Barbara says, "It should not be a crutch upon which to lean, but should be viewed as a valuable tool for guidance in your life."

My own respect for this craft comes primarily from observing the lives of people who have never spent five minutes thinking about it. Yet, as I compare their activities to their charts, planetary conditions seemed to be influencing their lives. Experience and investigation also lead me to believe that the more self-actualized or enlightened an individual is, the less these effects are felt.

It must be remembered that there are no absolutes in astrology—100% accuracy does not exist. Many of the most renowned practitioners in this country predicted as an absolute fact that President Ford would die in office. I've heard fifteen different rationales as to why they all missed on that one. The only explanation

I can accept is that they were interpreting strong potentials, not an absolute.

I consider this form of prediction irresponsible. It spreads unnecessary fear and needless mental anguish. A Phoenix astrologer once told Trenna that there was no way around the fact that her father was going to die in three months. Realizing that the aspects could be interpreted in other ways, Trenna knew enough to be objective about this prediction. However, she was still quite upset and worried the entire time. As it turned out, all the concern was unnecessary. Today, years later, her father is hale and hardy.

When such predictions are personal, it is always my concern that an individual will worry him or herself into the situation he or she desires to avoid. In dealing with astrology, I always advise people to remember one important fact: there is no influence greater than free will.

Chapter 14

PSYCHOMETRIC ATMOSPHERES

Places and Objects

For the gathering at the home of David Paladin, the subject of discussion was psychometry—the ability to divine facts concerning an object or a person associated with it, by contact with or proximity to the object. Several of the eighteen or twenty people attending this casual gathering brought disguised objects along with them. The objects, all small enough to hold in one hand, were wrapped and padded to make it impossible to identify the contents.

David Paladin is a nationally recognized artist with considerable interest in the psychic world. His home in Prescott, Arizona, is open every Friday to anyone interested in exploring and sharing psychic concepts. During this time, Trenna and I also lived in that mountain community, and we often enjoyed participating in the activities.

David explained the procedure. "Each of you can take turns holding one or more of the items. Simply blank your mind and trust the impressions that come to you. Then write them down on your paper."

I began deep breathing while sitting comfortably in a half-lotus position on the carpeted floor of Paladin's living room. By the time I received a padded manila envelope, I'd altered my state of consciousness to some degree. With eyes closed and my mind quiet, I began to get impressions of a girl with long hair standing by a lake. There were no further impressions, so I wrote down those I had received and passed the envelope on to someone else.

Trenna, sitting beside me, had also gone into a light self-hypnosis and was now busily writing an entire page about the bulky item she held in her lap. It was five by six inches around and appeared to be wrapped in many layers of newspaper.

It was interesting to observe that everyone had received impressions and was in the process of communicating them on paper. I remember the first time I'd seen the accurate use of psychometry in the 1960s. A local Scottsdale sensitive conducted private and group sessions in her small home half a block down the street from my office. She helped me solve my first dramatic encounter with the unknown and had exhibited her psychic abilities on several occasions after that. This was a period in which I was investigating everything in the Phoenix metaphysical community, which often included her Sunday evening sessions. Each Sunday, her small living room was filled with about twenty-five visitors, and she "read" for all who attended, using any of several different mediums.

One winter's evening, the technique was to be psychometry. We placed a question in a numbered envelop along with a personal article and our contribution. She would then call out our number and provide a three- to four-minute reading. Not seeking any particular information, my request was simply to read the impressions received from my ring. After listening to what seemed to be an endless flow of information about bad health and broken relationships (the primary reasons people go to psychics), she called my number and closed her eyes, holding the ring.

"I receive the strong impression of a girl with long dark hair. Her name starts with M . . . Maggie, Margo, or Meg. You share a relationship but she isn't here. She doesn't live in Arizona, but she will be here in August." There was additional, fairly accurate information, but it isn't pertinent here.

She was certainly correct on the name and physical description of a girl that was very important to me at the time. Meg lived in the Midwest, and our relationship was seemingly at a standstill, although at that time I would have welcomed her back into my life.

Nine months later, in August, Meg was in Scottsdale and tried unsuccessfully on several occasions to contact me. It worked out for the better, because I had been married in July, the month before. The psychometry reading had been correct, and the outcome beyond my ability to control.

David Paladin gathered the articles and began to open them. "Dick, why don't you read what you wrote?"

"It's quite short—'a woman with long hair in a white dress, standing by a lake.' "

David handed me a religious tintype of Jesus standing by a well. Obviously, I'd missed in some ways, but some portion of my mind had accurately perceived the long hair and robe, which I had interpreted as a woman in a dress. The well was hardly a lake, but water as one of the elements of the picture had been perceived. I was happily surprised.

Others who had held the disguised picture now related their impressions. Most participants were fairly accurate, showing at least a degree of psychometric ability.

Paladin unwrapped the object Trenna had held—a decorative ceramic chicken-and-egg figurine that looked as if it belonged on my mother's whatnot shelf. Trenna looked puzzled and nudged me, explaining that it didn't seem to relate to what she'd perceived. David asked her to read what she'd written.

"I see a small woman; she is elderly and has a cat. The cat is very important to her. She lost her husband in the war and has a son who lives quite far away. She spends a good deal of her time staring out of a kitchen window. She feels a great deal of peace here. She loves

130

to eat peanuts. She keeps them in a container by the window."

"I don't believe it!" exclaimed one of the other women in the group. "You have just described the woman who owns the figurine."

Most people in the group were accurate to some degree in their psychometric reading of the items presented. Some talked about the individual who owned the item, and some spoke of the items themselves.

Obviously, one of two things was happening. Either the physical/psychical emanations of the owners of these items had penetrated the items themselves, allowing a sensitive to read from them, or else the items created an extrasensory link between the owner and reader. Which explanation is valid is unimportant, for the result would be the same. The importance lies in a projection of the exercise: What does it mean on a scale of everyday living?

If enough time is spent in close contact with the object, an individual's emanations either penetrate it or become linked to it. Trenna and I were curious as to which objects were most effective in retaining emanations. We researched previous work in this field and conducted our own experiments. In the end, we agreed with earlier metaphysical investigators. Precious metals, such as silver and gold, will hold emanations longest, followed by other metals, ceramics and rocks, wood, paper, and fabrics.

Based upon our work with thousands of people, I am of the opinion that 20% of the American population is made up of "natural psychic sensitives." "Highly intuitive" would be another way to describe them. Very often, this empathic or psychic ability lies just under the surface, and the individual is not aware of it until he or she becomes quite involved in metaphysics. Everyone who opens the door to the psychic world is moving toward a state of psychic sensitivity. I'm referring to anyone who begins to read psychic and occult books, attends metaphysical meetings or seminars, or begins to practice any form of natural awareness expansion. These simple involvements open doors to power on the other side which will lead to the opening of the individual's third eye (psychic sensitivity). With proper knowledge of techniques and rites, the adept's sensitivity can quickly be developed into specific psychic abilities.

A psychometric atmosphere is thus a place or an object which becomes impregnated with etheric emanations that are consciously or subconsciously perceived by a sensitive individual. This results in an influence, but the neophyte will not realize why he feels these seemingly unfounded emotions.

Places: A mental atmosphere can remain as the focus of a manifestation of something physical that transpired in a particular location. A powerful emotion experienced somewhere will linger there almost indefinitely. An abbey, for instance, where Gregorian chants were performed for many years, might carry a mellowing magnetism. A room in which an alcoholic or a drug addict experienced acute mental pain might evoke fragmented vibrations.

Objects: A psychometric atmosphere can also accompany an inanimate object from the previous owner, reflecting his state of mind and level of awareness. For example, a used book on a highly charged subject such as metaphysics might carry considerable magnetism from the former owner, which could be undesirable if he was involved in witchcraft or was very troubled.

While lounging around the pool at one of Scottsdale's luxury apartment complexes, I was introduced to a middle-aged man in a red- and white-striped bathing suit. "You ought to talk to Richard about your situation, Eric. He investigates a lot of situations that are unusual," said Paul Rogers, our host for the afternoon.

"Do you really investigate people's strange behavior?" Eric asked me anxiously, extending his right hand. "Eric Rison, Richard. I'm glad to know you."

"I'm involved in psychic work and research in nutrition and naturopathic concepts," I explained after introducing myself.

"Can you tell me why a normally loving and warm woman would suddenly turn into an argumentative and spiteful person? Ever since we came here, my wife has been hateful to me and everyone else."

I used the standard psychiatrist's maneuver of looking right at him without commenting, so he would continue to talk.

"Martha and I have been happily married for twelve years, and we've always gotten along fabulously. Three months ago, we moved from Vermont to Scottsdale and are in the process of building our dream house out in the desert, but I don't know if we'll be together long enough to live in it. Martha and I are separated for a while. Not formally, but she went back to visit friends in Vermont."

"There are so many possibilities, Eric, it would take considerable investigation. My first inclination would be to have her check for a chemical imbalance in the body. Causes could be physical health, stress of the move, and responsibilities in building the new house, missing her old home, positive-ion charged winds which we've been having for a few months, or even the possibility of another man."

"Is your wife very intuitive?" Trenna asked.

"Very much so," he responded. "When the phone rings, she often tells me who is calling before she picks it up."

Trenna now turned to Paul and his wife Ellen. "Do you know anything about the couple who lived in the apartment before the Risons moved in?" They didn't, explaining that their apartment was on the other side of the complex.

"I know who could tell us," Paul said. "Jim, over there, lives a couple of doors down from Eric, and he's been here for at least five or six years." Paul invited him over and asked him Trenna's question.

"Sure, the Johnsons lived there until they got divorced a few months ago."

"Could you provide any details about their relationship or the divorce?" Trenna asked.

"Well, they say it's a thin line between love and hate,

and I believe it after watching that pair over the years. I sometimes think that they remained together just to takes turns hurting each other. We'd have to close our windows sometimes just so we wouldn't have to hear them screaming at each other. I don't think there is anyone in these apartments who was sorry to see them go."

"How long did they live there?"

"I'm not sure, but I think from the time the place was built. Their relationship kept getting slowly worse until it turned violent. He'd punch her, and once, she hit him with a vase. He had to have several stitches in his head. The last we heard, she had him arrested, and while the police detained him, she took the most precious possessions and disappeared."

I looked at Trenna and smiled, shaking my head and gesturing for her to explain to Eric.

"Eric, I really don't think that your wife is responsible for her actions. She is probably what we call an empath, someone who is psychically sensitive. She is capable of perceiving all the destructive emanations that still exist in your apartment. Years of negative energy have permeated everything in the rooms. The metal fixtures and appliances are probably holding the primary force, but since you moved in immediately after the other couple moved out, even the wallboard, wood, and flooring is magnetized with negativity. Your wife cannot help picking up the negativity and being affected by it. Talk her into coming back, but whatever you do, keep her away from that apartment."

"But something like that could happen in any apartment," Eric responded.

"It is a potential, Eric, but this sounds like a rather extreme case," I explained. We went on to provide him with a more complete explanation of psychometric atmospheres. He listened intently, and then excused himself to go call his wife.

"Considering her sensitivity, she could be affected anywhere," Paul commented. "Building a brand-new house that no one else has lived in is probably the best answer for them."

"Unless they build it on top of an Indian graveyard," Trenna reponded, thinking back to another situation in which the home occupants had been similarly affected.

"Oh, no! Let's change the subject," Paul said. "It's a beautiful day for a suntan and effortless conversation. I've been spooked enough for one afternoon."

Case History: Object

A seminar participant told the following story well after it had happened, but it is a perfect example of how the vibrations within an object can be an unseen influence. Betty LaCrusa is a thirty-two-year-old light-skinned Mexican American who makes her living as a craftsman in the Santa Fe, New Mexico, area. She does painting and silverwork.

"Being a silversmith, I naturally make most of my own jewelry," she explained. "But I've always been a nut for some of the old pawned work that you'll find in the better Indian jewelry stores and trading posts. I spotted an unusual Navajo bracelet, and I just had to have it. The Indian that had pawned it never returned to claim it, so the price was quite fair for such exquisite work. I purchased the bracelet and wore it often, probably three or four times a month. I'm an up person, and prior to this time, I can't remember any mental depressions in my life. However, I began to feel extremely depressed several times a month. Not just a little depressed, mind you, but *extremely* depressed. I couldn't figure out the cause, for there seemed to be no pattern to the depression at all. Sometimes, it happened when I was working at home; other times, when I was out on a date or having friends over.

"I had a physical checkup, only to find out I was in perfect health. I really became down because I didn't know when the depression would hit next—there was no pattern. This lasted for months, until a woman at a crafts fair noticed my pawn bracelet and inquired about it. I took it off and handed it to her. She was admiring its workmanship but quickly returned it, explaining that it was beautififul but had very negative vibrations. I didn't understand what she meant by that remark, so I asked her to explain.

" 'I'm a psychic from Dallas,' she said. 'I'm just traveling through on vacation. I feel very sad when I hold the bracelet. Have you had a tragedy in your life?'

"I explained that I hadn't but asked her please to tell me more. She said that she really couldn't elaborate on the subject because of the noisy fair area, but that if I wanted to come by her motel after dinner, she would attempt to psychometrize the bracelet for me. Now, I had very little understanding of the occult at this time, but something inside me said to follow through on this, so I went to the motel that evening.

"To make a long story short, the woman did some deep breathing, then closed her eyes and picked up the bracelet. She turned it over several times and clutched it tightly with both hands.

" 'I feel the presence of a very old man,' she said. 'I believe he made the bracelet . . . yes, I see him making it. I'm getting quick flashes. People dying. His wife first, of a sickness . . . accidents . . . his daughter was killed in an auto accident, and there is something about his son . . . he drinks . . . maybe . . . I don't know. There is no one to take care of the old man . . . he is hungry and sick . . . I can feel his hunger. This has been going on for a very long time.'

"That was the extent of the psychometry reading, but I never wore the bracelet again. I haven't been depressed a single day since then."

It became obvious in that seminar that Betty was an empath with extraordinary psychic sensitivity. Prior to her attendance, she felt she had no special psychic abilities, but her participation in several of the exercises and experiments proved otherwise. I explained that she should choose her environments, associates, and friends with great care, for she is perceptive on many levels and feels effects unnoticed by most of the world.

"Can't you exorcise away these influences?" is a frequent question. In response, I usually say that it can't hurt to try, but it doesn't always seem to work when you're dealing with highly empathic people. Yes, the bracelet could have been placed on newly spaded earth for a few days, which is the old way of demagnetizing an object. Yet, I'm not sure that this would have completely canceled out the long history of suffering recorded within the object. In the situation of Eric's apartment, an exorcism could certainly have rid it of unwanted discarnates, but negative emanations that have built up for years are another situation entirely. I've used white candles and sea salt for cleansing rituals, and I've watched other people perform their techniques, but I know of nothing that is totally effective for everyone.

Most people could have moved into the apartment or purchased the bracelet without experiencing any adverse effects at all, for they have no natural empathic abilities and have not purposely developed their psychic abilities. Yet, be aware that psychometric influences are in direct relationship to an individual's sensitivity. A slightly sensitive individual would experience a slight effect, and a highly sensitive person would experience a more extreme reaction.

Hundreds of people each year tell me that they want to develop their psychic abilities, and in response, my first question is: "Why? If your life is complicated now, I can guarantee you that it will be more complicated once you have opened psychically."

Chapter 15

ENERGY VAMPIRISM

Individual practitioners, such as psychologists, pyschia-
trists, hypnotists, astrologers, and psychics, will all
agree that sessions with some individuals are exceed-
ingly exhausting. It isn't that the people themselves
are troublesome, but only that by the end of the session, they have taken an excessive amount "out of us."

Over the years of my involvement with metaphysics,
I have twice worked on a daily basis as a hypnothera-
pist/counselor on individual cases. The first time, I was
director of the Hypnosis Center in Scottsdale, Arizona,
and a few years later, I worked in the Groom Creek
Mountains researching case histories for my writing.
It was during these periods that I came to understand
the term *energy vampirism.*

Trenna and I usually worked together with the subjects, and we compared notes on the aftereffects of a
session. Not once did we disagree about someone's
ability to suck our energy through "the big straw," as
we jokingly called it. Some people are givers; most
are neutral; and some are takers of energy. I've observed this phenomenon in seminar participants with
whom I've experienced less contact. Conversations with
the principals of three different New Age Seminar
organizations disclosed that we all shared the same
opinion, and no one could offer an effective way of

rising above the draining effect. It was a couple of years later that I found my way.

During the days of our individual counseling, Trenna and I often worked with other psychics in an attempt to break through a block in the subject's mind. After an all-day session with a midwestern couple, both Trenna and I could hardly walk from the hypnosis studio building back to our home, which was only a few yards away. Never had we been so drained of our energy by other people.

We were both aware that the problem wasn't the couple. It was one of the individuals. In this case, it was the man who was extracting energy from everyone around him, especially from his wife, who was in declining health. Usually, the energy vampire will derive most of the needed vitality from someone close to him —an individual with whom he has established a psychic rapport. This morbid attachment between two people can be found in any combination of individuals, but is most often seen in marriages and mother/daughter situations. Sometimes, it is witnessed in two female friends and on occasion between a mother and son. The individual who outwardly appears to be the stronger of the two is usually the taker, drawing support from the other. The giver is usually of sensitive temperament and often appears pallid and weak.

Cases in which the two have been separated to purposely break the rapport, the supposedly stronger individual usually shows signs of disturbance and outward weakness. The energy victim, on the other hand, usually begins to regain strength quickly if his or her mental health has not deteriorated beyond the point of return. You've probably observed such situations in marital separations or divorces. The stronger partner flounders, while the weaker quickly rallies.

Before continuing, I want to talk about life energies for a moment and then offer an experiment you can conduct at home to prove the existence of this unmeasurable human source of vitality. Kirlian photography is capable of capturing an aura of life energy on film. Cases have been documented in which a psychic healer and his patient have been photographed before and after a "laying-on-of-hands" treatment. Prior to the treatment, the healer shows a strong energy aura emitting several inches from his hands. The patient's energy aura is very slight. When photographed after the treatment, the energy auras are reversed. The photographs prove that the healer has actually transferred his energy to the patient.

In case you doubt the existence of this energy, you can easily make two energy-dowsing rods and prove it yourself. Find two lengths of sturdy wire about 18 inches long—a thin coat hanger is fine. Straighten out the wires and then bend a section at one end of each three inches long at a forty-five-degree angle. You are making handles to hold in your hands, while the main lengths of wire point directly in front of you. Your hands should be about six inches apart and at chest level. Next, have someone walk very slowly toward you, or you may approach them. As you get closer, the wires will move on their own and cross in response to the energy force of the other person. You will see that you are not moving the wires, but if you have doubts, put both wires in the same hand and watch them respond to the energy. It would be impossible to consciously manipulate this reaction.

Life energy exists. It can be transferred purposely or, as in the case of energy vampirism, without the consent of the giver. Possibly, some form of energy short-circuiting occurs in certain conditions or environments. In such cases, the stronger individual would be subconsciously absorbing the leakage instead of actively sucking it out. The term *psychic parasitism* might then be more apropos than vampirism.

Trenna and I worked with a woman in her late twenties who was an energy victim of her mother. Our subject was married and had two children, but her mother, who lived in the same city, drew her support from the daughter. Daily visits and follow-up phone calls were routine. The daughter's personality was passive. The mother's, however, was dominant, and she continually criticized and complained—if not about the upbringing of her grandchildren then about how her son-in-law should be a better provider.

The daughter was drained by the encounters, and her exhaustion began to show in her health and marriage. When her husband was offered a transfer to another city, she encouraged him to accept. The result was a new life of regained energy and positive outlook.

"What about your mother after you left town?" I asked.

"At first, her phone calls were far worse than when we lived in the same town. She got physically ill and complained so much that I couldn't take her complaints seriously. Maybe it was simply that I'd regained enough strength to improve my perspective, but I became much more assertive with her. Her doctor told her that she was run-down and put her on a diet and vitamin program to build her back up."

In the case of a certain married couple, I have the feeling that the wife intuitively knew what was going on in the relationship and thus acted to save herself without knowing all the details. Her husband was an extreme energy drain, not only to her but to anyone spending any time with him. A two-hour conversation with the man exhausted me.

The problem, according to him, was that after any kind of fight, his wife would leave for a week or two. This seemed to occur at about two-month intervals. Who started the fights? "They just seem to start on their own," he blustered. "But she gets all carried away and runs off to some relative's house every time." I never met his wife, but judging from my reactions, I believe she may have been leaving to recharge her batteries in an attempt to survive.

Nowadays, I do not allow myself to be affected by the energy vampires, but not because I have found a metaphysical technique to override the effect. Yes, you can use standard protective techniques, but I have yet to find any practitioner who claims them to be totally effective. If a practitioner makes such a claim, he must be actively involved with large numbers of different people. In conducting a seminar, there are aways people who want your attention at every break. They have a new question or problem, or they find some other excuse to gain attention. Invariably, this group is made up of the energy vampires in a seminar.

In the early days of conducting these sessions, I would often sleep for two days after a three-day seminar. I was drained as a result of openly giving my energy to all who sought it. After a few of these experiences, I began to use metaphysical powers of protection. I "charged" a large pentagram that was outlined on the stage floor with metal tape. During the sessions and the breaks, I remained within the pentagram, keeping others off the stage. The draining effects were mitigated to a high degree.

As the seminars evolved and I became more experienced, my way of handling the problem changed radically. Today, as part of the introduction to any group, I make the following statement: "I am not a guru. I don't believe in gurus. I can't help you. Only you can help yourself when you're ready to do so. In Zen Buddhism, the Master says, 'If you meet the Buddha on the road, kill him!' You see, we ourselves bring to life its only meaning. Any philosophy, technique, or truth that I might share with you is an empty idol unless you can apply it to yourself. To kill the Buddha is to destroy the belief that anything outside of yourself could be your master. No adult can be another man's disciple. I can't help you, and I don't want to help you. Don't tell me your 'PLM' (poor little me) stories, because I don't want the negative programming. Even if I could help you out of your situation, I wouldn't do it. To help someone else is often the worst thing you can do for him. Then he won't help his own self. He will never learn to be independent and capable. I'm not here to humor you, because that won't help. I'm here to share some concepts and techniques that will work to create a new reality if you're ready to put them to use."

By being direct and assertive, I eliminate 99% of the previously mentioned negative effects and am of far more value to seminar participants.

The two techniques for dealing effectively with energy vampires are to avoid contact with these people and to become assertive. Psychic protection techniques may provide some relief but will be far from satisfactory in most cases. I will discuss them in more detail in the next chapter.

Chapter 16

PSYCHIC ATTACK

I divide the concept of psychic attack into two forms: thoughts of others; and classical. Anyone can potentially be affected by either form, but one's level of psychic sensitivity will determine the degree of the effect. Those most affected will be the 20% who are natural empaths, and often they don't even realize their vulnerability.

Thoughts of Others

If someone close to you thinks negatively of you, those thoughts can affect your well-being. If there are several people thinking this way in a concentrated situation, such as a family or work environment, then it's even more probable that you'll be affected. Other people may not intentionally wish you ill, but their jealous or disapproving thoughts are projected. The more psychically sensitive you are, the more likely you are to be affected.

For example, imagine a situation in which eight middle-class housewives gather once a week for a neighborly coffee get-together. They are all frumpy and unattractive. A new family builds a much more expensive home on the only empty lot in the neighborhood, and the new woman is very attractive and has a good figure. She is invited to become part of the weekly event, and although the women are openly nice to her, they are privately jealous and resentful. The new woman is the subject of many catty conversations. The newcomer soon begins to experience periods of depression that she is unable to attribute to any cause.

Classical Psychic Attack

Classical psychic attack is the deliberate act of attacking another person by projecting negativity. The most common classical psychic attack technique, sticking pins in a voodoo doll, is simply a mental focusing device for the projection of thought forms. The same is true of many related voodoo rituals. There are now so many groups that teach mind control—Christian Science, Wicca, Mind Dynamics, Mind Control, Scientology, and my own seminars—and the information is intended to improve your life. I always stress the consequences of manipulation.

For example, I once received a phone call from a woman who explained that she continually felt bad and was unable to concentrate enough to work. A medical clinic had conducted every conceivable test without uncovering the cause. "Is there anyone in your life who really dislikes you?" I asked.

"Well, only my ex-husband. We were divorced last year, but he still hasn't accepted it," she responded.

"Has he ever taken part in any awareness or mind-control groups or organizations?" I named several, and she responded affirmatively to one of the names.

"That was his mother's religion, and he was in it for many years," she explained.

In such a case, I often suspect that psychic attack is involved. After regression sessions and psychic investigation were conducted, my suspicions were confirmed. A special protection tape, which she used daily, immediately ended the negative effects, and the woman returned to health and to work. When she later confronted her ex-husband, he admitted that he was purposely using techniques to "get even" with her for divorcing him.

Our investigations of psychic attack have proven it invalid in most cases. The real problems have often been:

1. An emotionally induced or psychosomatic disorder.
2. A personal manifestation of guilt or fear.
3. The result of subconscious negative self-programming over a period of time.
4. A difficult-to-define health problem, such as a chemical imbalance due to glandular problems or hypoglycemia.
5. Other unseen influences or a combination of these influences.

There is, however, strong evidence that psychic attack can be very real in some cases, especially for intuitive people or for those who are ill or mentally disturbed. Alcohol and drugs can result in vulnerability. Becoming involved in occult activities that are beyond your understanding, or being in a place where the forces are concentrated can mean exposure that results in negative effects.

In the third section of this book, I will talk about general techniques used to turn aside the effects of unseen influences. However, because psychic attack is a special situation, I will offer some specific methods for those who feel they are being victimized. In addition to using one or more of the protection and exorcism techniques described in this chapter, the following suggestions are valuable for anyone under attack:

1. Spend a lot of time in the sun. According to esoteric philosophy, the sun strengthens the aura and makes it more resistant. Do not fall asleep in the sun.
2. Refrain from all psychic/occult activities and reading.

3. Keep your psychic centers closed by eating well and often, every two or three hours.
4. Become mentally and physically involved in fun, materialistic things. See funny movies, play games, do physical training, interrelate with happy, positive people—in other words, keep your mind and body busy.
5. Seek to identify the source of the attack if possible so that you can exorcise any belongings that might relate to the individual.

Techniques

Cleansing of an Item: In the last chapter on psychometric atmospheres, I discussed how human emanations can penetrate an inanimate object. To demagnetize or exorcise the item, thereby breaking any inadvertent or purposeful vibrational tie attached to it, use either or both of these techniques:

1. Dig up and turn over some fresh earth. Lay the item on the ground overnight. The earth will absorb the vibrations.
2. Use the sea salt and water exorcism that follows.

Most occult practitioners use daily protection techniques as a matter of routine. Owing to their contacts and the nature of their work, it is a good insurance policy. Many envision themselves in a circle or bubble of protection and use a "mirror" method of reflection. If anyone projects negatively at them, it is immediately reflected back at the sender, resulting in quick karma for the perpetrator. The mirror aspect of the technique should certainly be considered from a karmic balance perspective before initiating it, but the technique is considered highly effective.

Trenna and I sometimes use a white-light technique before retiring. If either of us has had a recent bad dream or perceives any adverse influence in our environment, we intensify the protection by holding hands and combining the technique with hypnosis. On rare occasions, more powerful protective methods have been used. As public figures in the metaphysical world, we have received many letters from people who have informed us they were attempting to project astrally to our home. Since incorporating these techniques as a part of our daily lives, I have yet to experience a single incident in which someone has been able to project to us. Either the person's report is inaccurate and confused, or he has reported being "blocked."

The following are protective techniques using a white light that can be varied in many ways.

Circuit Sealing: If you find yourself in a situation in which negativity is being projected from another person, or you feel that someone is robbing your energy, imagine white light emanating from your heart area and surrounding you with a protective, magnetic aura. See it become a plastic bubble of protection from which you can see and hear the other person, whose emanations cannot reach you.

If you are in a position to do so, turn your body into a "closed circuit" in the following manner: Sit down and interlace your fingers, lay your folded hands upon your solar plexus, and keep your elbows pressed against your sides. Keep your feet touching each other. Your life energy cannot be drawn from you while you remain in this position.

White-Light Protection (Use with or without the candles, which tend to intensify the effect.): Light three white candles before going into meditation or hypnosis. Place one about a foot away from you on each side and the third the same distance from your feet. Now induce a state of altered consciousness and invoke the aid of your own guides and masters. Visualize a golden light coming down from above, entering your head, and beginning to flow through your body and mind. Sense it manifesting around your heart area and emerging from your heart as a bright, protective white light—a magnetic aura of protection that soon surrounds your entire body. The aura then begins to expand. Visualize this expansion very, very vividly. See the aura go out until it fills the room, then on out until it surrounds and protects your entire living quarters. See it as a protective white bubble. Then say these words out loud or in your mind: "The white-light protection is now complete, and any outside negativity directed at me from the physical or nonphysical realms will be unable to touch me in any way. All negativity, either purposeful as a psychic attack or simply the negative or destructive thoughts of others, will now bounce off this protective aura of white light like an image off a mirror. It will bounce off, and I ask that it be deflected out into space, where it will dissipate harmlessly."

Now create positive visualizations in which the psychic attack has ended and you are back to normal and feeling fantastic. Do this very vividly. Then say these words and complete the exercise before bringing yourself back to full consciousness: "I have now blocked all external negativity from my environment, and I desire to release all negatives within myself. This ancient technique is totally effective. I now release the negativity." (Blow out a deep breath, making an audible noise as you do so. Feel the negativity leaving your body and mind. Repeat the process three times.) "All negativity has now left my body and mind, and my environment is now positive and filled with love. I ask it and mark it, and so it is." An awakening process completes the procedure.

Rapport Breaking: A rapport, or telepathic connection, can be established with another person in any number of ways: personal involvement, sexual involvement, coexploration in altered states of consciousness, or close proximity in an office or home environment, to mention only a few. Brain-wave similarities between yourself and the other person would increase the intensity of the connection. A telepathic link between lovers, mates, parents, children, et cetera, might be desirable, but if it is an undesirable connection, it could influence negatively or even be vampiric (energy draining).

If you want to break a rapport, invoke protection in one of the previously mentioned ways. Go into hypnosis or meditation and intensify the protection. Then visualize yourself clasping a large Qabalistic Cross-handled sword in your right hand. You are holding it point upward. Now, visualize the tie that exists between you and the other person. See it as a ray of light or a shining cord emanating from your body and leading off toward his or hers. Now picture it quite clearly, and visualize yourself slashing down with the sword and severing the connection. Clearly imagine it bursting into a thousand fragments and dissolving away from you. Bring down the sword as many times as necessary to sever the connection in your visualization.

After this procedure, take the precautions necessary to prevent the connection from being reformed, as could easily happen. Do not see the victimizer and refuse to communicate or read any correspondence from him or her. Sever all physical contact as thoroughly as you have cut off the psychic one.

When speaking of making the sign of the cross, I am speaking of the Qabalistic Cross. This is equi-limbed—the cross of nature, not the Calvary Cross, of which the vertical shaft is double the length of the cross bar. The equi-limbed Qabalistic Cross represents:

The four corners of the globe.
The four elements.
The God Totality.

Sea Salt and Water Exorcism: Sea salt and water can be used in protective baptism, sealing a circle, or an exorcism. Salt is a crystalline substance, and to the occultist, it is the symbol of the earth element. Esoteric philosophy states that a crystalline substance will re-

150

ceive and hold etheric magnetism better than anything else. Water is used as the symbol of the psychic sphere.

On a table before you, place a container of fresh water and a handful of sea salt on separate plates. Light a white candle and visualize the expanding protective aura of white light.

Point with your first and second fingers to the salt and say, "I exorcise thee, creature of earth, by the positive powers of the universe (make the sign of the cross), by the God Totality (make the sign of the cross)." Extend your hand over the salt and say, "Creature of earth, I magnetize thee with the positive powers of the universe (make the sign of the cross) with the aid of my own guides and masters and the power of all those seen and unseen who share my energy (make the sign of the cross)." Point with your first and second fingers to the water and say, "I exorcise thee, creature of water, by the positive powers of the universe (make the sign of the cross), by the God Totality (make the sign of the cross)." Extend your hand over the water and say, "Creature of water, I magnetize thee with the positive powers of the universe (make the sign of the cross), by the God Totality (make the sign of the cross)." Cast the salt into the water and say: "I call out to the positive forces, to the protectory forces of light, to grant that this salt may make for health of body and this water for health of soul, and that the force we hereby create contains the power to banish every power of adversity, all negativity, and every illusion and effect of misdirected thought. I ask it, I mark it, and so it is."

The magnetized water may be used in a bath or for making the sign of the cross on the forehead or for making a protective circle through which no negativity may enter. You may also make a protective pentagram. When using the salt water, verbalize the following or a similar invocation: "In the name of all that is positive in the universe, and with the alliance of my own guides and masters, I exorcise all negative influences. To the perpetrator of these misdirected emanations, I send only love. From this time forward, all negativity will be deflected by this protection and will bounce out into space where it will harmlessly dissipate."

The aforementioned techniques are a basic arsenal of protection for most situations. As I said earlier, it is the psychically sensitive who need them. You can also combine the techniques with hypnosis or meditation and make your own tapes for induction and the verbalization of the proper wording. At one time, I made so many individual psychic-protection hypnosis tapes for individuals that I became tired of doing it. I cut the tape commercially in a studio so that it was readily available. Since then, several people have reported, "I'm so sick of your voice I could scream, but if I use the tape daily, I'm no longer affected by the problems I used to have." I always laugh and inform them that they don't need my tape and can do it themselves.

Is it actually the protection that is working, or is it one's belief in the power of the protection? Maybe it varies with the individual, but if all else fails in your attempt to rise above the unseen influences, you have nothing to lose by trying some of these techniques.

Chapter 17

OTHER INFLUENCES

The sixteen preceding chapters cover what I feel are primary influences affecting a large number of people, but there are many more. There are probably hundreds of additional influences that have helped to create your present reality and that are still at work behind the scenes. Light is a primary influence upon your well-being, and working under fluorescent lighting may be detrimental to your mental and emotional well-being. The radiation from color television sets has never been adequately explored. That tired feeling could be a mild case of radiation poisoning.

Basic environmental conditions affect people differently. There are geological patterns for the highest percentages of particular chronic diseases.

Chemicals in the water can also be unseen influences. As an example, in Oregon there is so much surface water due to the rain that residents' water needs are supplied from surface accumulation. They never draw upon the mineral-rich water that is deep in the earth. This results in a high incidence of dental cavities in that state as compared to others. A lack of essential minerals can have a great effect upon the individual who has a high need of a particular element that he isn't receiving. Many Oregonians may have had their health indirectly destroyed by a chain of cause and effect reactions linked to this simple environmental situation.

And so it goes. We realize that our knowledge is greatly outweighed by our ignorance. In some of the areas, such as body rhythms, there are only hints at answers. In health and nutrition, we are years away from having the necessary diagnostic techniques. We can drive our cars into computer-analysis garages and receive a print-out listing of everything that is wrong with it. Maybe someday, this sort of technology will be applicable to people—sort of computerized Edgar Cayce that can offer an individualized formula for optimum health and performance.

In the meantime, we must realize that there are no simple answers, no mystical techniques or cure-alls that will work for everyone. Each of us is an intricate balance of physiology, environment, and programming. All the elements interreact with each other, and every change results in a cause-and-effect chain. In attempting to offer a plan to rise above the unseen influences, I recognize my limitations, yet I draw upon extensive research and personal experience to present a four-step plan that offers optimum mental and physical health. I have shared this plan with many people prior to this writing, and *everyone* who has followed it has benefited. These four steps may not be all that you need to know, but if you follow them, you will change your life in many positive ways.

Section III

RISING ABOVE THE
UNSEEN INFLUENCES

Chapter 18

THE POWER OF THE MIND

At this point, you may be thinking: "My God, am I just a victim of circumstance—a puppet whose strings are being pulled this way and that? To what degree am I controlling my own life, and to what degree are external forces manipulating me?"

The answer depends upon your level of awareness and the state of your mental and physical health. You are a victim of destiny and negative circumstances to the degree that you avoid taking control of your life. A self-actualized individual experiencing optimum health and living a sensible life-style is far less likely to be adversely affected by external negative forces than most people.

Predestination is often a concern, because those interested in psychic prediction will usually have experienced a halfway accurate psychic or astrological reading in which the correct predictions were rationalized by the reader as an unseen force called "destiny." *Wrong!* The psychic was merely able to perceive a strong potential that already existed within you. It wasn't absolutely predestined, but there was such a high degree of probability that it was easy to predict. The key word here is *potential*. Let me provide you with a few examples to make my point:

1. If for the last thousand years, a glacier has been moving south at the rate of 6 inches per year, there is a very high potential that it will

move south another 6 inches this year. Yet, even the glacier's reality could be changed if there was an inverse ratio of snowfall to melt this year. Although a strong potential exists, it is not an absolute.

2. A businessman has been drinking more than he should for ten years and continues to drink a little more every year. Thus, there is a strong potential that he will become an alcoholic, and it follows that his health and personal relationships will also suffer. But the man could stop drinking.

3. A woman has been fighting with her husband for six years, and each year the fighting gets worse. Thus, there is a high potential that this momentum will continue, resulting in divorce when the astrological signs indicate an excessive weakness in this area. Yet, nothing is predestined, and wisdom could alter the reality. The problem is that most of us aren't wise enough to rise above our potentials, so we go through life flowing along with the natural current of karmic circumstances. These circumstances usually include many of the unseen influences.

As I have mentioned earlier in this book, the way to start creating a new reality is to change your way of thinking. If you accept your lot in life and believe the negative predictions, you will probably experience them. The same is also true in reverse. There is a saying among motivators: "Whatever the mind can conceive and believe, it can achieve." If what you conceive is within the realm of feasibility and programmed properly, I don't think you even have to believe it.

Free will overrides destiny, which is another way to say that the mind is *all-powerful*. If there is anything that my years of metaphysical investigation and psychic research have taught me, it is never to be amazed at the unlimited capabilities of the mind. It is generally agreed that we use no more than a few percentage points of our mental capabilities—maybe 5%. What about the remaining 95%? I am convinced that it is possible to contact a more knowledgeable portion of our totality that dwells in the mind. Call it the superconscious, the higher self, or god-self, there is an essence within us that is more aware than our waking consciousness.

Contacting the higher self is a technique Trenna and I teach in all seminars. You go into deep hypnosis and then use an additional technique to open a channel of direct communication with your own higher mind. Next, you send out a question and listen quietly as answers, and often visions, come back to you. Occasionally, I go into an altered state with a tape recorder running so I can verbalize the responses. I do not know exactly where the information is coming from, but it is often phrased differently from the way I would express it. Sometimes, I have received new information which was later verified.

Some of this information from the higher self has been used in previous books. Information that Trenna has received with this technique has served as gentle guidance for many important decisions we have made in our professional careers. The following question and answer communications are from my file labeled: The Power of the Mind (Metaphysical Questions).

Dick's question: There are many books and organizations which relate the experiences of individuals who have contacted the other side. Some general concepts are consistent, but there are far too many inconsistencies for an objective investigator to accept. The founder of one well-known metaphysical group had an out-of-body journey and found a multileveled nonphysical world governed by different gods. Other groups talk of similar levels, but there is no agreement at all on details. One says there are five, another seven, and each group designates different names for the levels. There are rays and guides and Sanskrit terms, and every organization has its own esoteric dictionary. If you compare the words of psychics, channels, and researchers, you find the same problems—they do not necessarily agree with one another. What is nonphysical reality after death all about?

Answer: All is mind. Each person experiences or glimpses his totality in a way that relates only to himself. If he keeps it to himself, he has had a psychic experience; but if the experience is published in a book or used as the foundation for an organization, there will always be joiners eager to accept it as truth. It was a symbolic truth to the man who experienced it, but that certainly doesn't mean that it relates to anyone else.

Dick: Symbolic truth?

Answer: There is no such thing as truth with a capital *T*. One religion is not right while the rest are wrong. One belief is not closer to the truth than any other. Truth exists only as it relates to yourself. You ask whom to listen to and whom to believe. The only answer is: "Yourself." If you see the other side as five levels which you must work your way through, then that is what you will find at death. If you see it as a burning hell, your mind can also arrange for that. How about a mountain environment with creeks stocked with trout? All is mind. As you have often said, Richard, "You do not have a mind; you are mind." The answer is that there is no answer at all except creativity. Entities exploring in the physical world are overpowered by that degree of freedom; thus, they create elaborate belief systems to make themselves feel secure, and they cling to others who share their concepts as an additional crutch.

Let me ask you a question: Which of these three visions would you be most likely to relate to—an angel, an Indian woman, or an extraterrestrial spaceman?

Dick: An Indian woman, because I feel that vision relates to my reincarnational lineage.

159

Answer: All right. Let's say that another portion of you, call it your higher self, decides to communicate with the conscious "you" that is now lying there on the bed. The Indian woman vision would be a good medium to get your attention, would it not?

Dick: Yes.

Answer: But the man down the block would think of an Indian only as someone who wandered off the reservation. He could not relate to this vision. He might not accept an angel as anything but a hallucination, but a UFO or an extraterrestrial entity would be something worthy of sitting up and noticing.

Dick: But it would not be there?

Answer: Not necessarily.

Dick: How do you explain a situation in which several people see the same thing, such as a religious apparition? Let's take the 1961 case of the four young girls in San Sebastián de Garabandal in northern Spain. All four girls simultaneously went into ecstasies when the angel appeared. Tests showed they were all in trance and exhibited no reaction to physical pain. Each girl reported the same communications from the angel and Blessed Virgin, who also appeared, and it created a sensation in the religious world. Although thousands of people journeyed to the village to observe these regular occurrences, the apparitions were seen only by the girls and a thirty-six-year-old priest, who died a few hours after the experience. Those who observed the girls in ecstasy had no doubts as to the reality of their experience. Eventually, it was only one girl who continued to communicate with the Virgin. In 1965, she was told that a worldwide chastisement was forthcoming, but it would be preceded by a warning that would be visible all over the world. There would be a great miracle which would take place at Garabandal. The sick who were present at the miracle would be cured, and the sinners converted. The Virgin then explained that she had to go away, and that there would be no more contact.

Answer: The answer can be summed up in one word: mind. Some apparitions are valid projections from one individual to another. Some aren't. Some people can "project" an effect. Their minds have the power to function as a "reality projector," although they don't consciously realize it. They will be as amazed as everyone else at what they are observing, but they created the apparition and projected it to those attuned to their vibrational field, such as close friends or others on their frequency. The common frequency could have been created by the common belief system. Apparitions are usually the result of a very deep belief system. Combine your knowledge of the Catholic Church and sensitive young girls, and then assume one girl has an exceptionally strong mind with extrasensory projection capabilities. You already understand the subtle possibilities of group hypnosis in a case like this one.

Regarding the predictions which have not come to pass, you must realize that this is a standard pattern in such occurrences. The principals become consciously or subconsciously carried away by the mystical manifestations, but when something inside them realizes that they don't have the power to expand the effect, the apparition says good-bye, and the prediction does not come to pass.

Dick: So, if I saw the Indian woman, she would only be a creation of my own mind or of someone else's mind?

Answer: I will answer yes, and then qualify my answer by saying that all is perspective. You might be dreaming in an altered state of consciousness or manifesting the reality through mental projection, or the energy essence (mind) of the Indian woman is projecting to you. After all, a nonphysical entity is pure mind. So you must project the physical form, nationality, and clothing. If you'll notice, there are very few people discussing naked apparitions, for they even project their own proprieties into their visions.

Dick: But could an Indian woman who has died contact me?

Answer: Yes, under the proper conditions.

Dick: Then how would you judge the experience?

Answer: If you must judge, I would do so by what was gained in the experience. Of course, if you have to have proof, as in the case of the girls in Spain, you could judge by the validity of the promised effect: the miracle.

Dick: How do you explain situations in which people see the future when it does not directly relate to them? A psychic seeing President Kennedy being shot. An avalanche burying those children in Europe, et cetera.

Answer: There is no single answer. It would be generally accurate to say that sensitives were reading potentials, but there are other explanations. Remember that even among the nationally famous psychics, predictions of this type are highly inaccurate. People forget about all the misses. If you have any doubts, dig out the January first issues of some of those supermarket tabloid newspapers. [I did, and found that the only accurate hits had to do with increased inflation and a few celebrity divorces.] These psychics are much more accurate when they work with individuals. Then they can read potentials directly from the minds of their clients.

Extrasensory perception certainly exists, and someone who has developed his ability in this area can read potentials more accurately. President Kennedy was hated and feared by many people during a time of turmoil. Thus, his potential for assassination was high. There were hundreds of different assassination predictions for many different times. Yet, the woman who is credited with trying to warn him to not go to

Dallas incorrectly prophesied the outcome of a following presidential election.

As another example, a psychic in California told your friend Katie that she would be riding her horse and the horse would hurt his foot. As it happened, her daughter Jane was riding the horse when his foot was badly cut by a piece of barbed wire. Thus, the prediction was partially accurate. Katie had previously perceived the wire on one level of her mind but never gave it any conscious thought. The horse was so important to her that it remained in her mind as a "charged" thought of potential danger. Since she went riding in the same area every day, the potential for the accident was always there. The psychic perceived the potential and verbalized it. Psychics are apt to perceive input that is emotionally charged, because it stands out in the mind. Thus, predictions of relationships, of joy, pain, and important experiences are most common.

Remember, Richard, when the Arizona psychic told you that your close friend in Minnesota had just had some difficult health problems, and you later found this to be true? I'm sure you now understand that since you and your friend were close, you were in superconscious communication. Thus, you perceived important data from each other on a level above consciousness. The psychic simply took the information from your higher mind via extrasensory perception.

You see, each situation is different, but each one can be explained by the power of the mind. Everyone can develop these abilities if willing to take the time to do so. Out-of-body perceptions are often the explanation for a psychic experience. A man sleeping in the United States wakes up in a cold sweat because he dreams of an avalanche killing an entire lodge full of children. In the morning on the radio, he hears that the event actually took place. The probable explanation is that while his mind was traveling (astrally projecting) as his body slept, he was drawn to the situation by the terrible anguish that created a charge perceivable to anyone on the astral plane. He didn't dream the event; he observed it.

There are also other explanations for psychic experiences, such as time warps, or "jumps," but this phenomenon is unusual.

Dick: All right, let's move on to another area —the power of the mind to heal the body.

Answer: To say that the mind has the power to heal the body is incorrect. The mind has the power to help the body heal itself, but there is obviously a point beyond which it cannot alter a deteriorating effect. Mental power in healing is a matter of relativity. Drugs never heal the body; only the body can heal itself. Drugs or mental programming set the stage for the body to begin self-healing.

Dick: What about the time David Paladin was scheduled for open-heart surgery, but he used psychic healing techniques that worked, thus avoiding the surgery? Or Robert's ability to eliminate the cancer in his body with self-hypnosis healing techniques?

Answer: There are good examples of aware individuals using the power of their minds while there was still time to do so. Had either condition progressed a little farther, this might not have been possible. Ideally, both men, after eliminating the problems, eliminated the conditions which weakened the body to allow these physical problems to develop. A positive mental attitude, no excessive stress, a proper diet, and exercise will enable a body to ward off most illness. This life-style will certainly accelerate self-healing if any problems do develop.

While the mind is using the physical body during an incarnation, each is affecting the other in a coexploration. Your mind expands and grows as the result of a healthy body, and your body's peak performance comes through mind power.

Dick: Do you mind if I quote that line?

Answer: How could the higher self mind if his lower self quoted him?

Dick: Lower self? I'm not sure I like that term. Who am I really communicating with in these sessions?

Answer: Who do you want me to be?

Dick: We could go on like this for a long time, couldn't we? Instead, let's communicate about the concept of mental reprogramming.

Answer: You're already a specialist in that subject. What exactly are you asking?

Dick: I explain it to people from a technical perspective. How would you explain what happens when someone uses hypnosis techniques to create a major change in his life?

Answer: The physical world is a reflection of your mind. As an example, take a man who grew up in abject poverty in a big city. From his youth, he felt that he didn't belong in such circumstances and envisioned owning a little house and a secondhand automobile. To achieve such a condition was a dream that would place him far above his peers. Today, this is his reality—he owns a $45,000 house and an old car. Had he spent years dreaming of a $150,000 house and two new cars, he probably would have achieved that goal.

People feel they belong in certain circumstances, and the mind reflects their belief system in reality. Even if an individual loses everything, he will quickly find a way to reconstruct the envisioned environment.

Most people will tell you that they want more than they have or that they desire to alter certain circumstances. However, they don't really feel they deserve better, or they subconsciously fear the results. Thus, nothing changes. Reprogramming is a way to concentrate new pictures in the mind so that it begins to reflect a different reality.

Dick: Thank you for the sharing.

Answer: Anytime.

Chapter 19

A FOUR-STEP PLAN TO RISE ABOVE THE UNSEEN INFLUENCES

If you incorporate into your life-style the following four-step program, it will change your life in many positive ways. This is not a probability; it is an absolute. You will change for the better, becoming a healthier, more positive, secure individual. It has never failed for anyone. However, this is not a plan you can use for a month to achieve results before drifting back into old habits. This plan is a permanent life-style.

Today, when people come to me seeking help in overcoming the unseen influences, I hand them this plan and suggest that they begin work on the unseen after they improve themselves mentally and physically. No one has ever come back for more help, although many have sent thanks.

One: Programming

If you don't plan a direction in life, you have made a choice—that of *no choice*. If you have no goals or specific directions, you can be assured that you will flow right along the river of destiny, experiencing the potential results of your past programming. If that doesn't appeal to you, the first step toward self-improvement is to decide what you want in life. What are your short-term personal and social goals? Your long-term personal goals? Your professional goals? What do you want to be doing three years from now? Six years from now? Ten years from now? If you can't answer these questions, you have no right to be disappointed when you're unhappy with your present situation.

If you have trouble establishing your goals, look back upon your life. In retrospect, what are the highlights? These can be good clues for the future. Fantasies are also good clues. Commit your goals to paper, remembering that you can create any reality within the perspective of your background and potential experience, as long as it doesn't require manipulation of someone else. You simply have to be willing to pay the price, which could be time, effort, perseverance, or risk. Naturally, you must be responsible to your goals by educating yourself in keeping with the desire. The chapter on programming dreams provides complete information about how this programming works.

Once you know what you want, begin daily self-hypnosis programming. In *Past Lives, Future Loves,* I explain the self-hypnosis process in step-by-step detail, using suggestion and mental movies. In addition, I explain how to make your own hypnosis tapes. Other books on the subject are readily available, as well as prerecorded self-hypnosis tapes specifically prepared for reprogramming. Hypnosis can often be learned in community college classes and specialized seminars. Although I won't repeat the explanation in this book, I will provide you with some background on hypnosis.

Hypnosis/self-hypnosis is a technique used for self-programming, self-exploration, or relaxation. It can benefit anyone. It is the ultimate means of heightening motivation by programming your subconscious mind to work in cooperation with your conscious desires.

Self-hypnosis is a technique any reasonably attentive individual can learn. People with very low IQs, neurotics, and very young children are not good subjects, for they have short attention spans.

When I am speaking publicly, people often ask me if it is possible to become dependent upon self-hypnosis.

My response is that nothing could be further from the truth. Hypnosis has no physical or permanent effects upon the body or mind. There isn't any way to become dependent upon it. I do know that a lot of people look forward to their daily self-hypnosis sessions. They become entirely relaxed, and they awaken refreshed and ready to go, feeling better than before they went into an altered state of consciousness. You might say that I'm dependent upon it in the dentist's office because I don't like pain shots. Quick self-hypnosis completely blocks the pain of the drill.

In addition, it's impossible to hypnotize anyone against his or her will. Even after a hypnotic state is achieved, you can hear, talk, think, act, or open your eyes at any time. You realize that you are not unconscious, but you feel very relaxed. Let me outline what I consider the most important basic facts about hypnosis.

1. Directly proposed hypnotic suggestion cannot make you do anything against your morals, religion, or sense of self-preservation. If such a suggestion were given, you would either refuse to comply or would wake up.
2. The ego cannot be detached under hypnosis, so you will not reveal any secrets while in a trance, and you won't do anything you would not normally do if you felt relaxed about the situation.
3. The best hypnotic subjects are intelligent people. The more strong-willed and imaginative you are, the greater your potential as a hypnotic subject.
4. There are many overlapping levels of hypnosis, but for the sake of simplification, I will break them down into three:

   A. *Light Trance:* You become very relaxed, although you probably will not feel that you are hypnotized. Most people easily achieve this level.

B. *Medium Trance:* You become totally relaxed and are completely open to suggestion. You can feel or relive any suggested event. You may be aware, to a degree, of what is going on around you, but it will not distract you from the hypnotist's voice.

C. *Deep Trance:* One person in ten achieves a somnambulist level. You become completely relaxed and respond easily to standard hypnotic depth tests. You will not remember what you have experienced while under hypnosis unless specifically commanded to do so upon reawakening.

5. Self-hypnosis is a learned technique. You do have to work at it, and if you are willing to work daily for three or four weeks, you will become a well-conditioned subject.

6. Anyone can be hypnotized. Once an individual overcomes his apprehension by understanding the truth about hypnosis, it is an easy experience. You will reawaken feeling more relaxed, at ease, and at peace than before going into hypnosis.

7. Unless you are in a deep-level trance, you will remember everything that you experience while in hypnosis. If you are very tired, you may fall off into a natural sleep—not hypnosis.

8. Most people do not recognize the state of hypnosis. They expect to become unconscious. Unless you are the one in ten who easily achieves the deep-level trance, this is not at all what the experience is like. The chances are that you will remain aware of everything going on around you. This does not mean you are not hypnotized; it simply means you are experiencing a hypnotic level somewhere between a light and medium trance. The experience is different for everyone, but normally you go into a slightly deeper trance each time you

undergo hypnosis, until you achieve your "natural level."

9. It is desirable to darken the room or use a dark sleep mask when working with hypnosis. This is certainly not necessary, but it does seem to make visualization easier for most people.

Two: Aerobic Exercise

For all of us, a sedentary life-style will eventually result in declining health. It is that simple, and there are no exceptions. A body that isn't used deteriorates. The lungs become inefficient, the heart weakens, the blood vessels lose pliability, the muscles lose tone, and the body weakens overall, resulting in the entire delivery system for oxygen losing its effectiveness. Vulnerability to illness automatically follows. If you compound this problem by smoking, drinking, overeating, or worrying, you probably won't be around long enough to worry about a new reality unless you make some immediate changes.

If you want to maintain health, then exercise. If you want to regain health, then exercise—but not just any old exercise. It must be aerobic. The word *aerobic* means "with oxygen," and aerobic exercises build endurance, the best kind of health insurance. They demand oxygen without producing an intolerable oxygen debt. Your lungs begin to process more air with less effort, and your heart becomes stronger and pumps more blood with each stroke, reducing the number of necessary strokes. Aerobic exercise also increases the number and size of the capillaries that carry the blood to your body, thus delivering more energy-producing oxygen. Muscle tone is improved, often resulting in reduced pressure. These facts are now well substantiated by millions of people who have followed the advice of Dr. Kenneth H. Cooper, one of the first developers of an aerobic fitness program. Since 1971, Cooper's clinic has evaluated 10,000 patients. The plan is used by the U.S. Air Force, other services both in this country and abroad, cardiac clinics, athletic organizations, medically organized corporation fitness programs, and local YMCAs. It is age-adjusted, so regardless of your present age and condition, unless you are very sick, you can start now.

The primary aerobic exercises are:

> Walking
> Jogging
> Running
> Bicycling
> Swimming

Other activities that can result in aerobic points are:

> Cross-country skiing
> Rope-skipping
> Stationary cycling
> Stair-climbing
> Rowing
> Disco dancing
> Golf
> Tennis
> Badminton
> Skiing
> Volleyball
> Fencing
> Handball
> Racquetball
> Squash
> Basketball
> Soccer
> Hockey
> Roller-skating

Although many exercise programs are built upon one of the following exercises, none of these will replace aerobic activity: isometrics, calisthenics, and weight lifting. Yoga is an ideal combination exercise to use *with* aerobics, but it cannot offer the cardiovascular advantages and increased lung efficiency of aerobics.

An aerobic exercise is one that is vigorous enough to effect and then sustain an accelerated heart rate. The benefits begin about five minutes after the increased heart rate and continue as long as the exercise is performed. It is from this prolonged pulse increase that the benefits are derived. If the increase is not sufficiently high but the exercise still demands oxygen, it must be continued longer.

The specifics are worked out in the chart system of Cooper's aerobic plan, and you can find it in any bookstore, health club, or athletic center. Some doctors now distribute this information. Many published doctors agree that exercise is even more important than nutrition, although ideally, you will combine the disciplines.

Three: Diet and Nutrition

I'm not going to pull punches on this step to avoid being labeled a radical or to provide a dietary plan that is more acceptable to the masses. Nutritionists throughout the world wholeheartedly agree with this approach to diet and nutrition, for it is the optimum plan available. You will accept it or you won't. You may have to take it step-by-step, but anything less than what is presented here misses the mark.

The following foods destroy health and should be completely avoided:

1. White sugar, or any refined sugar/sweetener, and everything made with it.
2. White flour and everything made with it.
3. Coffee, standard tea, chocolate, and all soft drinks, including diet drinks.
4. Tobacco and alcohol.
5. Salt, black pepper, and mustard.
6. Canned, preserved, frozen, and irradiated foods.
7. Meat.

Although this list looks overpowering at first glance and almost eliminates the supermarket, any investigation will reveal that plenty of delicious and healthful foods remain. Numerous cookbooks and dietary information are available at most bookstores and all health food stores. The following suggestions will help you to regain and maintain your health:

1. *Your Basic Diet:* Vegetables, whole grains, nuts, seeds, fruits, and dairy products, such as eggs, yogurt, and cheese. To the extent that you are able, make sure you are buying natural foods grown in fertile soil and without chemicals and other artificial means.

2. *Eat Whole Foods:* Complete, unrefined foods are superior. Examples: 100% whole-wheat bread (read the ingredients label and make sure they haven't added enriched wheat flour and sugar as most do), potatoes in the skin, oranges rather than orange juice.

3. *Eat Living Foods:* Grow your own sprouts and eat salads, nuts, seeds, fresh fruits, and vegetables. Ideally, at least half of your diet should consist of poison-free raw food.

4. *Eat a High–"Natural" Carbohydrate, Low–Animal Protein Diet:* This is the diet of all nations which are known for good health and longevity. Fish may be eaten if you desire.

5. *Sweeteners:* Small amounts of honey or fructose only. Fructose looks and tastes like sugar but does not stimulate insulin from the pancreas to the degree that sugar does.

6. *Drinks:* Fruit juices, herb teas, mineral water, milk, and kefir.

7. *Undereat:* Stop eating before you are full. The amount you eat is as important as what you eat. According to the insurance company charts, you will be healthiest several pounds under your desired weight.

8. *Megadose Vitamins:* Because America's soil is deficient in vitamins and pollution widespread,

it is important to take daily vitamins in quantities that maximize your protection. All people are different, so there is no correct amount for everyone. Following are the minimum and maximum amounts recommended by four of the primary nutritionists. **However, before adopting any kind of vitamin plan, you should absolutely check with your doctor and obtain professional advice.** Without medical supervision, any vitamin program could be potentially dangerous as each person has individual needs and tolerance levels. We can only make suggestions and do not offer professional medical advice on vitamins.

If you are not now taking any supplements, it would be best to start with the minimum and slowly work up to the maximum over several weeks' time. Use natural, rather than synthetic, vitamins.

A good daily vitamin supplement and a B-complex pill will cover many of the requirements. **Vitamins A and D can be toxic in quantities above these recommendations. Don't take vitamin E and your iron supplement at the same time. Spread out your intake over your three meals.**

Vitamin A	10,000 IU to 25,000 IU*	
Vitamin D	400 IU to 1000 IU	
B-complex: B1	50 mg to 100 mg*	
B2	50 mg to 100 mg	
B6	50 mg to 200 mg	
B12	100 mcg to 750 mcg*	
Vitamin C	1500 mg to 4000 mg	
Niacin (B3)	50 mg to 250 mg	
	(will cause flushing)	
Niacinamide	100 mg to 250 mg	
Calcium	300 mg to 600 mg	

---

* IU=International Units; mg=one thousandth of a gram; mcg=one millionth of a gram.

PABA	500 mg to 1200 mg
Vitamin E	200 IU to 800 IU
Pantothenic Acid (B5)	50 mg to 150 mg
Folic Acid	2.0 mg to 3.6 mg
Magnesium	10 mg to 40 mg
Zinc	15 mg to 75 mg
Choline	300 mg to 750 mg
Inositol	400 mg to 1000 mg
Biotin	150 mcg to 300 mcg
Rutin	45 mg
Bioflavonoids	300 mg to 500 mg
Iron (Ferrous Fumarate)	10 mg to 18 mg
Iodine (kelp)	50 mcg to 225 mcg
Potassium	10 mg to 100 mg

In addition, the following is also suggested: B15 (Pangamic Acid), lecithin, garlic capsules, ginseng, brewers' yeast, and selenium if you live in a selenium-poor section of the country. The Midwest from the Dakotas through Texas, and the Southwest are rich in selenium, but the rest of the country is poor, especially the East and Pacific Northwest.

For additional information, I recommend *Are You Confused?*, by Dr. Paavo Airola, *The Main Ingredients: Positive Thinking, Exercise and Diet*, by Susan Smith Jones, Ph.D., *Super Nutrition*, by Richard Passwater, and *Know Your Nutrition*, by Linda Clark.

The Hunzas, living in the Himalayas, are known to be the healthiest and most long-lived of any people on earth. After reading several volumes written by scholars of the Hunza people and listening to tape recordings of another researcher, I believe that their health secrets can be summed up very quickly.

1. They eat a diet such as I have just described.
2. They live a quiet life filled with plenty of relaxation, and they sleep from dark to dawn.
3. Exercise is a way of life for the Hunzas, as

they are farmers who work the fields by hand. The men and women climb steep terraces to go to and from the fields.

4. There is minimal stress, for they live in a communal environment of mutual help.
5. They do not drink alcohol, but do drink a rock-resin tea that contains all the necessary minerals.
6. This life-style means good elimination, which is a primary necessity for a healthy, youthful life. The bowels should move three times daily, with the well-formed stool being a sign of constipation.
7. The Hunzas live in an unpolluted mountain environment.

Four: A Self-actualized Perspective

Self-actualization: a personal philosophy of becoming all that you are capable of being and a perspective of involved detachment in which you accept all the warmth and joy of life, while mentally detaching from the negativity. You maintain high self-esteem and a sense of peace regardless of circumstances. You rise above external manipulation and fear and achieve environmental unity.
—Dick Sutphen

The fourth step of the plan is to work toward the establishment of this philosophy. If you achieve it, you will end your tensions and turmoil and begin an integrated and self-fulfilling life: Let's examine self-actualization one part at a time.

A personal philosophy of becoming all that you are capable of being: Most people never begin to live up to their potential in life. They attempt to win races driving a car with a governor set for 35 miles per hour, while they are capable of removing the governor so the car will do 120. You can remove the governor and begin to program the reality you want to live.

A perspective of involved detachment in which you accept all the warmth and joy in life, while mentally detaching from the negativity: Let's relate this concept to a man/woman relationship situation. Your husband is kind and loving, and you accept and fully enjoy every moment of the warm times you share. Yet, when his work is overpowering, he becomes short-tempered, thoughtless, and selfish. At these times, you simply let his words go in one ear and out the other without affecting you. You become stoic.

People feel that a problem is not solved unless it is eliminated. *Perspective is the primary solution to most problems. When you are no longer affected by a problem, you no longer have a problem, although nothing about the problem situation may have outwardly changed.*

Here are some examples:

1. Your husband grouches at you every morning at breakfast. You are upset by it, and your entire day starts off badly. *Change your perspective:* Realize that it is his right to grouch, but it is your right to pay no attention. It is foolish to allow someone else's lack of balance to upset your balance. When you have evolved into a self-actualized individual, the negativity will automatically be rejected. Until then, program yourself to be unaffected by such things. In this situation, when you cease to be affected, you will no longer have a problem, although the situation remains the same.

2. You frequently become irritated by the traffic jams going to and from work. *Change your perspective:* There is nothing you can do about them, and your anger only makes for negative programming of your subconscious computer and will later result in more negative life experiences. Everything in life is a value judg-

177

ment. You could move, work elsewhere, or do any number of things to avoid this traffic situation, but of course you would then have to make other concessions. Realize that you have chosen this situation as part of the best solution for now.

3. Your mother-in-law says: "You are really a thoughtless person. I don't see what John ever saw in you in the first place." You react with hurt and anger. You allow your day to be ruined and will probably take your anger out on your husband when he comes home. *Change your perspective:* It isn't what somebody says to you that affects you. It is what you *think* about what they say to you that affects you. A more appropriate reaction would have been to allow the statement to go in one ear and out the other. Or you could have used an assertiveness training response.

You maintain high self-esteem: Self-image is critical to your happiness, success, and freedom. If you think you're a leader, you'll act like a leader; but if you think you're a dummy, you'll act like a dummy. I have written much in this book about how your thoughts program your reality similar to the way a computer is programmed. From that perspective, the importance of self-esteem is obvious. A key point to remember is that what you do in life equals your self-esteem. Thus, one of the reasons that accomplishing goals is so important is that it reinforces your self-esteem. Anything that causes you to lose self-esteem is unacceptable. For example, let's assume your neighbor wants to borrow your car. You don't want to lend it but are reluctant to say no. If you say yes you lose self-esteem, and when this event is combined with other similar situations, you eventually program an undesirable future.

You maintain a sense of peace regardless of circumstances: Your basic perspective as described up to this point will allow you to look at all situations with an involved detachment resulting in a relaxed state of mind. In martial arts, the student is taught: "Keep your mind like calm water, thus reflecting accurately the image of all objects within range. If it is necessary to fight, you will perform most efficiently with a calm mind and without anger."

You rise above external manipulation and fear: Fear is the only problem that exists between people. Tension, frustration, anxiety, indifference, guilt, insecurity, selfishness, inhibitions, and possessiveness are all emotions rooted in fear. The wife who admonishes her husband because he flirted with another woman at a party is exhibiting possessiveness due to fear of being ignored or fear of loss. She is indirectly saying that she wants him to change, to be a certain way. One country goes to war with another country because it wants more land and control; it is fearful that it doesn't have enough. Think about it, and you will see how all problems between people relate back to fear in one way or another.

When you learn to rise above the effects of fear, you release the limitations of your belief system. One of the best ways to surmount fear is to establish a code and perspective by which to live. I will offer what I call "Eleven Human Rights." They allow for expression, rather than repression, and are the ground rules for assertion. Any self-actualized individual will gladly grant these rights to others, while demanding them for himself.

Assertiveness is the expression of your own rights, needs, feelings, and wants. If you are not standing up for your rights, you have little freedom and you're functioning from an uncomfortable and fearful internal basis. In the long run, you will damage your relationships, mental and physical well-being, and self-concept. Behavioral psychologists report that those who have acted nonassertively for long periods of time usually have a poor self-concept. The individual who stands

179

up for him- or herself and takes initiative reduces anxiety and increases his or her sense of self-worth.

Assertion is commonly mistaken for aggression, but understand that to be assertive means that you are standing up for your basic human rights. Aggression is a matter of forcefully violating the rights of another, and there is no excuse for such behavior.

An important part of assertiveness is showing consideration for the feelings and rights of others, without letting your kindness or empathy be used as an opening for manipulation. Realize that background conditioning has made everyone good at manipulation, and people will use your vulnerability as an opening. The better they know you, the better they know your vulnerable areas. The assertive individual becomes an expert at expressing his rights, needs, and feelings in a kind way, and he shows equal respect for the same rights, needs, and feelings of others.

People often avoid being assertive because they feel others will dislike them if they speak up and say what they really feel. That is not a rational justification for allowing yourself to be manipulated. If by any chance, someone did stop liking you because you said no, are you going to miss their friendship? Your friend was only a puppet master, and nobody needs that sort of control in his or her life. If you are one of the millions who go through life thinking that a wrong word or a refusal or an assertion is going to end a relationship, it is time to realize that is simply not how things work. Such thinking is usually based upon such a strong need to be liked that you sacrifice your own self-respect, often without realizing it. You probably also fail to distinguish between being liked and being respected.

As an assertive, self-actualized individual, you give and take more fairly than ever before, thus being of more service to yourself and others. You become relaxed about revealing yourself through your words and actions and begin to communicate openly, directly, and honestly with the people in your life.

ELEVEN HUMAN RIGHTS

1. It is your right to do anything if it does not violate someone else's human rights and if you are willing to accept the consequences.
2. It is your right to maintain your self-respect by answering honestly, even if it does hurt someone else—as long as you are being assertive as opposed to aggressive.
3. It is your right to be what you are without changing your ideas or behavior to satisfy someone else.
4. It is your right to strive for self-actualization.
5. It is your right to choose your own priorities.
6. It is your right not to be subjected to negativity.
7. It is your right not to offer excuses or justifications for your decisions or behavior.
8. It is your right not to care.
9. It is your right to be illogical.
10. It is your right to change your mind.
11. It is your right to defend yourself.

This list amounts to this simple summary: Live your life doing things either because you want to do them or else because, as a personal value judgment or compromise, you have agreed to do them. Any decision resulting in loss of self-respect is unacceptable. Do not do things because they are expected of you or because you think you should or because you will feel anxious or guilty if you don't.

Now, let's examine the eleven rights a little more closely.

It is your right to do anything if it does not violate someone else's human rights and if you are willing to accept the consequences. This ancient axiom is one of the basic assumptions of numerous esoteric philosophies and belief systems. It is considered by many to be the one commandment by which to live. Critics call it selfish and hedonistic, but they are only looking at the surface. It does not say that you shouldn't help others or be kind and considerate and loving. It does say that you are a free individual who has the right to do anything that doesn't harm someone else.

Obviously, in exercising your rights, you realize that personal value judgments must be part of your decisions.

If you were to leave home for a week without telling your husband where you were going or when you were coming back, he might worry about you, and thus, you have hurt him. But if you tell him you can afford a vacation and your responsibilities are covered, you have a different situation.

As another example, if after discharging your self-accepted household duties, you decide to go sit in the park for the afternoon, you certainly shouldn't have to explain where you were or what you did. Value judgment is the key word. If your husband is extremely possessive and demands knowledge of your every movement, he might not be willing to accept being denied the knowledge of your whereabouts. If your assertiveness results in a punch in the nose, nothing will have been gained. Thus, if the relationship is extremely close and carries a high value priority, you may want to start practicing assertion in low hostility areas with the goal of creating a more satisfactory life-style.

As another example, let's say you are a fairly good painter, and you decide to show your work with a local art association one Sunday a month. You win a best-of-show award, but your husband is not enthusiastic about your success. He soon begins to work against your participation. He may feel insecure for a number of reasons: you are getting recognition, you are doing something on your own, you might meet interesting men. However, you are doing something that is creatively fulfilling, and you are certainly not hurting anyone

182

else. In a situation such as this, unless there are extenuating circumstances, you should assert your rights.

It is your right to maintain your self-respect by answering honestly, even if it does hurt someone else—as long as you are being assertive as opposed to aggressive.

For a moment, imagine yourself in the following situation:

Your Mother: I have a big dinner planned for the entire family this Sunday, so you, John, and the children should come over about one.

You: We can't do that, Mother. We're going to rent a cabin in the woods this weekend.

Mother: Well, I have this all planned. You can rent a cabin another weekend.

You: We could rent the cabin another weekend, but I want to go this weekend.

Mother: You mean you'd rather go to an old cabin in the woods than make your mother happy by coming over to her house for dinner?

You: This weekend I would rather go to the woods. Another weekend I might prefer to have dinner with you, Mother.

All right, your mother is now hurt because she put herself in a "choose between me and something else" contest, and you chose something else. It was a manipulative attempt to use guilt by oversimplifying the decision—your mother's happiness versus an inanimate bunch of boards in the woods. Obviously, that wasn't at all the basis of the decision. You handled it in a kind way by offering the compromise of coming for dinner on another weekend. If your mother chooses to be hurt, she must deal with her feelings. Chances are, she's simply frustrated that you aren't willing to play the old manipulation game with her.

The key word in this particular right is *self-respect.*

A phony excuse or an unfelt apology will cause you to lose your self-respect, and that is never acceptable.

It is your right to be what you are without changing your ideas or behavior to satisfy someone else. No one can change someone else, nor should anyone expect another person to become anything other than what they are. Any forced change either will not last or will result in new eruptions of unsatisfactory behavior. We are all free human beings and should be respected for what we are, not for what someone else wants us to be. If your behavior makes someone else uncomfortable, he has the right to leave. The same is true for you.

Often in a close relationship, one person will compromise in hopes of achieving harmony. He or she will change; thus, the other person is now reacting to a different (changed) person. Often, this person will also change. In this sort of situation, the change is natural and will probably last.

It is your right to strive for self-actualization. You have the right to become all that you are capable of being in all areas of your life. A self-actualized mental perspective is an involved detachment by which you are able to accept all the positive aspects of life, while allowing the negatives to flow past you without effect. As one example, let's project the concept of self-actualization into an ideal man/woman love relationship. In such a situation, your love could not be diminished by anything the other person says or does, because you wouldn't allow any negativity to register. You would realize that other people's actions do not affect you. It is your thoughts about their actions that affect you. You would realize that anytime you were emotionally upset, you were at fault for allowing someone else's lack of balance to affect your balance, for allowing someone else's problem to create a problem within you. Also, your love would not be dependent upon being loved. You would give freely, without any expectation of return. In an environment of self-actualized love, you would allow complete freedom to your mate, expecting no more than he or she could give. You would love the other for his or her intrinsic self, never expecting a change. You would find joy in the other's happiness. You would have risen above fear and beyond problems.

Most of us are still striving for self-actualization, but it is a goal within the reach of all. Assertiveness is a major step toward this ambition.

It is your right to choose your own priorities. Ask your mate, children, parents, in-laws, and friends what they feel your priorities should be, and I'm sure you'll get many different answers. No one else can relate to your position and know what is best for you or what you should do. It is your value judgment as to what you will do with your time and in what order you choose to accomplish your tasks. It is also your right to choose whether to accept any responsibility for another's problems.

For example, your relatives expect you to help out when Aunt Nellie breaks her leg and cannot get around. Now, you and Aunt Nellie have never liked each other. She is very rich and can easily hire help to do menial household tasks.

You: You'll have to find someone else to help Aunt Nellie.

Relative: But each of us is going to spend a week at her house, and you're the only one who has said no.

You: Well, I may be the only one that has said no, and that is my decision.

Relative: Some people are really uncooperative when it comes to helping.

You: I do believe in helping people, and I am unwilling to spend a week with Aunt Nellie.

Often, it is service people who attempt to place responsibility on your shoulders. Let's assume your bank did not enter a deposit into your checking account, and you have been notified that two checks were returned. You go to the bank teller and demand that she find the missing deposit and credit your account immediately.

Teller: We can't do that right now. When Sally comes back from her break, she will attempt to clear it up, and we'll call you later today.

You: I want someone to rectify it immediately so that no more checks are returned.

Teller: Well, there are a lot of people waiting in line to be serviced. (The teller is now attempting to induce guilt by implying that you have some responsibility to see that the bank is able to serve people without making them wait.)

You: I do seem to be holding up the line, so I would suggest that you quickly rectify the bank's error in my account so these people won't have to wait even longer.

It is your right not to be subjected to negativity. Negativity programs the computer portion of your brain, the subconscious. If your resistance or level of awareness is down, negativity can be contagious. No one should be judged harshly for unwillingness to remain in a negative environment.

Your friend has been crying on your shoulder about her marriage problems for the last year. Now she is separated, contemplating a divorce. It looks like the situation could go on indefinitely.

You: I understand that you are having a hard time, Donna, but hearing about it affects me in a negative way. I'm no longer willing to discuss your problems.

Friend: I don't understand. You know the whole awful background, and I've always leaned on you in crises.

You: I realize that you have leaned on me in

crises, but it affects me, too. I'm no longer willing to be affected.

It is your right not to offer excuses or justifications for your decisions or behavior. In asserting yourself, you may want to explain your feelings to those with whom you share a close relationship, but you don't owe them an explanation. When asserting yourself to people who are not close to you, explanations and excuses weaken your statements and position. Avoid using the word *but* and other qualifying words that weaken your position.

You to your boss: I cannot work overtime tonight, and (instead of *but*) I can come in before working hours in the morning if that will help.

You did not apologize or offer an excuse, but you did offer a workable compromise in your willingness to come in early.

You to a salesclerk: There is a money-back guarantee on this product if the buyer is not satisfied, and I am not satisfied. Please refund my money.
Salesclerk: What is wrong with it?
You: I'm ~~not~~ satisfied. Please refund my money.
Salesclerk: Yes, but what is wrong with it?
You: I don't have to explain to you what is wrong with it. I am dissatisfied, and I want you to refund my money.

We all find ourselves in positions in which others imply that we owe them explanations. Most of us are so well trained that we react automatically and comply with their wishes without thinking. All too often, we explain ourselves even when no one has asked us to.

It is often hardest not to offer an explanation to a good friend, but why should a friend force you to explain your behavior? If your friend is incapable of accepting your assertive rights, then maybe he is incapable of relating to you on any basis but manipulation.

It is your right not to care. Life is filled with *you-shoulds*. You should improve yourself. You should care about all 500 of the charity operations in this city. You should care about banning the bomb and Aunt Nellie's broken leg. Your mother is getting old and is worrying about her age, so she thinks you should be concerned about old people in general. The PTA thinks you should attend monthly meetings, and the FCC thinks you should be concerned about violence on television. Your husband thinks you should roll his pairs of socks together instead of dumping them in a heap in the dresser drawer. There are so many *you-shoulds* that if you did, you'd have no time left for anything else. You, and you alone, decide what to care about.

It is your right to be illogical. Logic usually works well in science, but in human reationships, it is often used as a manipulative ploy. Because logic usually implies superior judgment, it is an effective control technique. Here are two examples:

"We can't go to the movie tonight, because we have to get up early tomorrow." That statement sounds logical, but from your perspective, missing an hour of sleep won't stop you from getting up early.

"We can't put in new shrubs if we expect to put a new picture tube in the color TV." From your perspective, you'd prefer the new shrubs *and* the picture tube, but you'd be quite happy to eliminate the new kitchen table for which you have allocated funds.

It is your right to change your mind. People change their minds, and thank goodness they do. Otherwise, we would be a very rigid society, and all the men would still be wearing crew cuts. What works for us today may not work tomorrow. What you liked last year may not fit with the more aware you of today. Or maybe you just got tired of living that life-style and changed

188

Changing your mind is healthy and normal, but other people may resist by challenging your right to do so. They will want explanations and the admission that your first choice was a mistake. "How can you change your mind after you committed yourself? You're irresponsible and will probably make a faulty decision next time."

It is your right to defend yourself. Obviously, it is your right to defend yourself from any threat of physical violence. If the threat is verbal, however, it might be wise to hold back your immediate response until you see whether you're merely defending your need to be right. In that case, you may get to be right—and lose the game. You always have the right to respond to verbal aggression with assertiveness techniques.

You achieve environmental unity: This is the last portion of the original self-actualization definition. Environmental unity is divided into two aspects: people and places.

People: Eliminate negativity from your personal environment. This advice includes negative people. As you become more positive, you will be unwilling to listen to or remain in the environment of those who are negative. Listening to others moan, groan, and complain is detrimental to you, for it is programming input. Changing your perspective will help, as I discussed earlier, but if your friends or relatives cannot relate to you in any way other than through negativity, why remain in their environment? Sometimes, the only way to be responsible to yourself is to remove yourself from the negative environment. "If you want to be happy and successful, surround yourself with happy and successful people." The self-actualized individuals whom I know don't have a lot of friends. There are not many truly positive people that will be assets to their lives. Those they call friend, or family in a larger sense, are close and important. For the most part, though, self-actualized individuals are self-fulfilling; they live internally more than externally and thus require fewer people.

Places: Create an environment in which you find peace. This could be a room, a house, or a geographical location. Be aware that value judgments are the only barriers between you and the environment you desire. And the happiness you feel within your environment will reflect in all other aspects of your life.

I have introduced you to concepts in the areas of programming, exercise, and diet/nutrition. This information should be the beginning of additional exploration on your part. The four-step plan I advocate is simple, though not necessarily easy. There is no doubt that the plan works, so it is up to you to exert the discipline to put it into effect. You can continue to flow along with your destiny, or you can take it into your own hands. I sincerely hope you're ready for that responsibility.

ABOUT THE AUTHOR

Dick Sutphen is an author and innovative hypnotist who specializes in regression and reprogramming. His best-selling books, *You Were Born Again to Be Together* and *Past Lives, Future Loves* (Pocket Books), have become metaphysical/self-help classics. In the past four years, he has appeared on over 300 radio and television shows.

Working with his wife Trenna, Dick conducts several reincarnation and human-potential seminars each year. The couple also direct Valley of the Sun Publishing, which offers a large line of hypnosis tapes and publishes a quarterly magazine called *Self-Help Update*, which presents the Sutphens' latest research.

The Sutphens reside in Malibu, California. Address inquiries to: Dick Sutphen, Box 38, Malibu, CA 90265